D0965422

Psalms Now

PSALMS
NOW

Leslie F. Brandt

SAINT LOUIS

BS
1440
.B73
1996

OTHER BOOKS BY LESLIE F. BRANDT

Jesus/Now
Epistles/Now
Meditations/Now

Copyright © 1974 Concordia Publishing House.
Revised copyright © 1996
3558 S. Jefferson Avenue, St. Louis, MO 63118-3968

Manufactured in the United States of America

All rights reserved. No part of this publication may be reproduced, stored in a retrieval system, or transmitted, in any form or by any means, electronic, mechanical, photocopying, recording, or otherwise, without the prior written permission of Concordia Publishing House.

Library of Congress Cataloging-in-Publication Data

Brandt, Leslie F.
  Psalms/now / Leslie F. Brandt.
    p.   cm.
  ISBN 0-570-04257-7
    1. Bible. O.T. Psalms—Paraphrases, English.   I. Title.
BS1440.B73   1996
223'.205209—dc20   96-14857

1 2 3 4 5 6 7 8 9 10   05 04 03 02 01 00 99 98 97 96

FOREWORD

The Book of Psalms is a miniature Bible, a miniature history of God's people. It expresses all the feelings and experiences they will ever have.

John F. Brug
People's Bible Commentary: Psalms II

Perhaps the best–known and best–loved book of the Bible, the Psalms have long held a central position in the spiritual life of believers. From the original authors to the modern reader, the Psalms express our emotions, our desires, even our faith, to our heavenly Father. As one person has said, "We were born with this book in our very bones."[1]

Originally written as personal or community expressions of worship, countless generations have used the Psalms to convey "the whole range of human emotions in their relation to God, from extreme pessimism and doubt to simple and certain trust."[2] Psalms were assigned for each Jewish festival and temple ritual. Some of these prayer–poems may have been written for the coronation ceremonies of the Israelite kings. Other psalms were much more private, communicating personal, heartfelt needs, sorrows, or joys. Every possible human experience and emotion is addressed in this book of 150 poems, including salvation, bondage, illness, healing, birth, death, joy, depression, anger, and thankfulness. And the list grows with each new reading and each new life event.

CONCORDIA UNIVERSITY LIBRARY
2811 NE HOLMAN ST.
PORTLAND, OR 97211-6099

The child Jesus probably first heard and learned the psalms from His parents and then continued to study them as an integral part of His formal education in the synagogue. The New Testament indicates that Jesus and the apostles were well–versed in the Psalter—the most–quoted Old Testament book in the New Testament. In fact, the disciples and Jesus probably sang psalms often—even on the night Jesus was betrayed (Mark 14:26). The apostle Paul instructs the early Christians to include the psalms in their worship (see 1 Corinthians 14:15, 26; Ephesians 5:19; Colossians 3:16). Today, we continue to use the psalms for public worship (as litanies, Scripture readings, prayers, and in hymn form) and for private devotions.

But why have such statements as "The Lord is my shepherd" or "God is our refuge and strength" or "Create in me a pure heart, O God" remained timely for the modern reader? How can these ancient songs of praise, petition, lament, and joy still be relevant? Perhaps it's because the Hebrew writers communicated a depth of emotion with which we all can identify. William Swan Plumer, a 19th–century clergyman and Bible scholar, found that, when his spirit was "excited, or devotional, or sad, and [seeking] an echo to its enthusiasm, its devotion, or its melancholy," he turned to the Psalms.

> There I find words which seem to issue from the soul of the ages, and which penetrate even to the heart of all generations. ... Read Greek or Latin poetry after a Psalm, and see how pale it looks.[3]

When God's Holy Spirit directs our reading and studying of the Psalms, we see reflected back to us the sin that separates us from God (Psalm 51) and God's perfect plan of salvation fulfilled in Jesus that erases that sin and binds us to Him (Psalm 22). While Martin Luther first realized the truth of justification by faith from his study of Romans, his study of the Psalter reinforced his new understanding of the "righteousness of God" (Psalm 85).

Brandt's poetic restatements of the Psalms explore our contemporary relationship to God.

Luther came to see the righteousness of God not as the threat of God's righteous judgment against sinners but as God's grace and mercy in Christ. "The `righteousness of God' is that through which the righteous lives by the gift of God ... through which the merciful God justifies us by faith."[4] Thus, Luther found that all the Scriptures pointed to the sweet Gospel message that God has worked salvation for us and gives it freely.

Luther found in the Psalms strength and inspiration for his struggle with the Catholic church. He and his circle of friends often sang Psalm 46 when feeling overwhelmed. Indeed this psalm, on which Luther based the Reformation anthem "A Mighty Fortress Is Our God," is known as the psalm of "holy confidence" for God's people.[5] Luther not only found inspiration in the Psalms for many of his hymns, he spent significant time

7

studying the Psalms, lecturing on them, and reading them for his own personal spiritual growth. Luther commented:

> With this book I have occupied, delighted, and trained myself from my youth, and, thanks be to God, not without great benefit. Yea, I would not exchange the blessing of the Holy Spirit which I have obtained by enjoying and considering the psalms for all the thrones and kingdoms of this world. [6]

Another explanation for our love of the Psalms may exist in Jesus' love for the Psalms. The Gospels record numerous references to the Psalms. At His Baptism, the voice from heaven echoed the words of Psalm 2:7, "You are my Son; today I have become your Father." Several Beatitudes find their beginnings in the Psalms (for example, "Blessed are the meek" echoes Psalm 37:11). The crowds that welcomed Jesus to Jerusalem before His death cried out "Blessed is He who comes in the name of the Lord!" (Psalm 118:26). As Jesus hung on the cross, He cried out "My God, My God, why have You forsaken Me?" (Psalm 22:1). And after His resurrection, Jesus opened the minds of His disciples to understand how all Scripture, including the Psalms, pointed to Him as the Christ, the promised Messiah (see Luke 24:27, 45—47). Peter even quoted the Psalms in his great Pentecost sermon (Acts 2:25—28, 34—35). And the early church continued to incorporate the Psalms in their worship, always reading them with a messianic ear. In these ancient songs, the new believers found the truth of God's promises in Jesus Christ.

We only need to look at one psalm, Psalm 23, to see how central the entire book is to our spiritual life. As one commentator says:

> This Psalm has sung its way into more hearts
> than any other part of the Bible except the
> Lord's Prayer. ... The tiny tot memorizes it
> before he can read, and the old man dies with
> it upon his lips.[9]

And William Plumer adds his admiration for the poet King David as he asks, "Where else do we find a whole Psalm expressive of personal confidence, joy, and triumph from beginning to end?"[8]

If the Psalms are the "faith of the Old Testament set to music"[9], than Psalm 23 is the apex of this Old Testament hymnal. Here David carries his praise beyond thankfulness for a specific act of salvation to "a confession that God will always exercise personal care ... . The psalmist ... does not simply pray for this but claims the certainty of enjoying it."[10] In Jesus' words that He is the Good Shepherd, we come full circle to realize that God has delivered us from the evils of sin and this world and leads us to quiet waters and green pastures. From its first singing until the present, Psalm 23 "has dried many tears and supplied the mould into which many hearts have poured their peaceful faith."[11] Psalm 23 will continue to uplift believers and provide the assurance that God does walk with us, even carry us, until we reach His eternal banquet table.

If the original Psalms are still speaking to today's Christians, why do we need a paraphrase such as Psalms/Now? Because this paraphrase provides Christians with new ways to celebrate the promises of protection, victory, salvation, light, and life God offers us through the words of the Psalms. Brandt's poetic restatements of the Psalms, rooted in the emotions and faith of the ancient songs, explore our contemporary relationship to God. These modern poems help us understand that we can, in our own everyday language, praise God, plead with God, question God, even yell at God.

Brandt says in his preface that he has spent years reading the Psalms, finding in them ways to "articulat[e] my feelings and verbaliz[e] my prayers as a struggling saint." He has offered this paraphrase as one way to "honestly and openly express ... doubts and perplexities to the living God" so that we can "lay claim to God's promises and demonstrate our faith." These are the very things the original psalm writers sought. Their songs expressed the depth of their emotions and faith in their heavenly Father.

The Psalms, whether in a "modern" paraphrase or the original, should have a distinct place in our devotional life, a place that reflects their witness to Christ as Lord and Savior and their remarkable "capacity to express the character of the individual's relationship to God."[12] Each of us can, as Brandt has, adapt the Psalms to address our own joys and concerns. Using the biblical text as a guide, we can give voice to our own personal prayers and praises and give God the glory due His name. And in those moments when words fail us, we can call to mind the soft reminder that the Lord is our shepherd, the sweet assurance that His love endures forever, and then join "everything that has breath" in praise of our great God.

The Editor

1. A. Chouraqui as quoted in The Psalms: A New Translation (Westminister Press, 1963).

2. J. W. Rogerson and J. W. McKay, The Cambridge Bible Commentary: Psalms 1–50. (Cambridge, Great Britain: Cambridge University Press, 1977), 2.

3. William Swan Plumer as quoted in The Treasury of David, Volume 3, by Charles Hadden Spurgeon. (Grand Rapids: Zondervan, 1966), 465.

4. Ewald M. Plass, comp., What Luther Says. (St. Louis: Concordia, 1959), 1226.

5. Debb Andrus, comp., God's Word for Today: Psalms. (St. Louis: Concordia, 1994), 11–12.

6. Martin Luther as quoted in Studies in the Psalter, by O. W. Wismar. (St. Louis: Concordia, 1926), 1.

7. Arnold B. Rhodes, The Layman's Bible Commentary: The Book of Psalms. (Richmond: John Knox Press, 1960), 51.

8. William Swan Plumer as quoted in The Treasury of David, Volume 1, by Charles Hadden Spurgeon. (Grand Rapids: Zondervan, 1966), 357–358.

9. Rhodes, 8.

10. Patrick D. Miller Jr., Interpreting the Psalms. (Philadelphia: Fortress Press, 1986), 119 (emphasis added).

11. A. Cohen, The Psalms. (London: The Soncino Press, 1950), 67.

12. Miller, 21.

PREFACE

I first read the Book of Psalms through at the age of 10. I don't remember what they said to me at that time, but in the ensuing years they often articulated my feelings and verbalized my prayers as a struggling saint. In the 20th year of my ordained ministry, I began to "rewrite" a few of them for my church bulletin. These were eventually published in three small volumes and later were all included in a single book, *Psalms/Now*. Now, more than 20 years later, this present volume has been revised. The language speaks to both young and old, male and female, longtime Christian and newcomer to the faith.

I am expressing what the Old Testament psalmists might be saying if they were approaching the 21st century. The name *Christ* is not used; the Messianic import of the Old Testament psalms is not noted. Yet these prayers are voiced by those on the Christian side of the Easter event—believers whose every approach to God must be by way of God revealed through Jesus Christ.

Today's Christians, like the ancient psalmists, can honestly and openly express their doubts and perplexities to the living God. And as we do this, we can lay claim to God's promises and demonstrate our faith in celebration of His presence in the world today. If these psalm-writing efforts help make the ancient psalms more relevant for modern saints and if they help express more adequately the perpetual conflicts of a child of God in our complex society, they will serve their purpose.

1

Those persons who choose to live significant lives
       are not going to take their cues
          from the religiously indifferent.
Nor will they conform to the crowd
       nor mouth their prejudices
          nor dote on the failures of others.

Their ultimate concern is the will of God.
They make their daily decisions in respect to such.
Compare them to a sturdy tree
       planted in rich, moist soil.
As the tree yields fruit,
       so their lives manifest blessing for others
          and are purposeful and productive.

This is not true concerning the ungodly.
They are like sand in a desert storm
       or leaves in an autumn wind.
They cannot stand against the judgments
       of the eternal God.
And they are most uncomfortable
       among those who demonstrate genuine faith
          in the God of righteousness.

The children of God walk in the course
       that God has ordained.
The children of unbelief walk
       in paths of self-destruction.

2

Why do dictators and governments
    throughout our world
    persist in persecuting the people of God?
They may be divided in everything else,
    but they unite in their endeavors
    to free themselves from the restraints of religion.

Disconcerting as this is to me,
    our great God laughs at their foolish efforts.
And His laughter will have the sound of fury
    in the day He determines to act against them.
He will reveal to them who truly is Lord and King.

But to me, even in the midst of my confusion,
    He speaks as a loving Father.
"You are My child and servant," God says.
"Trust in Me; I control the
    destiny of the world.
You shall overcome;
    you shall frustrate their attempts to destroy you."

So wise up, you who sit in high places.
Begin serving the God you are trying to silence.
Bow your hearts in submission
    before He crowns your heads with divine wrath.
Only those who rest in God's will are truly secure.

3

O God, so many obstacles confront me today!
And even as they press in upon me,
    there are people around me
        who laugh at my childlike dependence on You.
They claim that my faith is futile,
    that God is not interested in my petty problems.

But, God, You have surrounded me with Your love.
You envelop me with concern
    and undergird me with grace.
When I reach out for You,
    You are close enough to hear and to respond.

Whether I am awake or asleep,
    You are near me and watch over me.
I do not have to be afraid
    of these problems that assail me.
The conflicts of my life will not separate me from You.

I constantly seek Your deliverance
    from all that hurts or hinders.
You are able to rid my life of everything
    that may threaten my relationship with You.
You will, in Your own good time, set me free
    from every human fault and frailty.
But even while I await Your ultimate deliverance,
    help me sense Your presence and power
        in the midst of my many conflicts.

4

Dear God, respond to Your servant in distress;
    make room for a disciple in despair;
    listen to the agonizing cries of a child
        who is depressed and unhappy.

O you who I thought were my friends,
    why do you keep hacking at me,
        gloating over my errors,
        rejoicing at my failures,
        always looking for the very worst in me?

I must remember that I truly do belong to God,
    that He does feel for me when I hurt.

Go ahead, explode, cry out, or complain;
    it doesn't frighten God,
        but guard that you don't hurt anyone else.
Then, O foolish heart, simmer down
    and renew your confidence in God.

I hear voices around me
    whining about the wickedness of the world,
    begging for divine demonstration of might and right.
And yet I know I have discovered
    more delight in my relationship with You, O Lord,
    than they in all their possessions and pleasures.

And so I can lie down and sleep in peace.
Because of You, I am eternally secure.

5

Can You hear, O God, what I have to say?
Do You feel something of what I feel this morning?

I know, O God, that You are grieved
    by the selfishness of Your children.
The world You created seems to be falling apart.
Your creatures are living for themselves alone,
    proud and self-sufficient.
They think they don't need You any longer.
I also know, O Lord, that I cannot exist
    without the assurance of Your eternal love.
Thus I commit myself once more to You and Your purposes.
Help me walk in Your path for my life.
Give me grace to overcome the many obstacles.

The philosophies that come out of our world
    bear little resemblance
        to the truth You revealed to us.
These subtle, seductive worldviews
    lead people astray
        through forked tongues and suave soft-sell.
Enable us to recognize them for what they are:
    shallow, superficial, ultimately destructive.

Those who follow You need not be dismayed.
They can sing and dance in the joy of their Lord.
You will continue to reveal Yourself to them
    and care for them and work out Your purposes
        in and through them.

6

O God, don't clobber me in disgust
     or chastise me in anger.
But the fact is, I'm falling apart.
I am distraught and confused.
I am in deep trouble,
     and I don't know how long I can take it.

I can only beg You to enter into my conflict,
     to extricate me from this incessant battering,
     to demonstrate Your love
          in deliverance and salvation.
Otherwise I'm going down the drain;
     and how, then, could I either praise or serve You?

I am fed up with this continual agony;
     I can no longer endure these perpetual defeats.
I am becoming increasingly discouraged
     about my human frailties and fallibilities.

If only I could be sure
          that You know about my anguish,
          that You discern my cries for help,
          that You also feel and understand,
          that You will never let me go.
Then I could stand firm even in defeat
     and rise victorious even over my failures
     and make even my human weaknesses
          serve You.

7

O God, I come running to You
   like a frightened child.
My pursuers, like hideous monsters,
   seek to tear me limb from limb.

O Lord,
      if I really am to blame for their hostilities,
      if I have willfully hurt anybody,
      if I have selfishly blighted another person's soul,
         then let the ax fall;
      I have no right to live;
         I almost wish I could die.

O God, have mercy.
You know the secrets of my heart
   and the desires of my flesh.
You know I want so much to do Your will.
You know my greatest enemy is myself,
      how ineffectual I am
         in dealing with my inner conflicts.
You know, and You have assured me, that You care.
You have judged my wickedness;
      now rise up to deliver me
         from its ugly consequences.

Oh, when will there be an end to evil?
When will this frustrating struggle cease?
I claw like a wounded animal
   at the promises of God for comfort.
I appeal to His love for solace and strength.

I know the end of those
   who do not repent of their sins.
Their selfishness boomerangs; sin kicks back.
They stew in their own juices.

Thus I must run to God in my defeats
   that I may learn to walk with Him in His victories.
I will continue to sing His praises
   and to lay claim to His righteousness.

8

O God,
    how full of wonder and splendor You are!

I see the reflections of Your beauty
    and hear the sounds of Your majesty
        wherever I turn.

Even the babbling of babes
    and the laughter of children
        spell out Your name in indefinable syllables.

When I gaze into star-studded skies
    and attempt to comprehend the vast distances,
I contemplate in utter amazement
    my Creator's concern for me.
I am dumbfounded that You
    should care personally about me.

And yet You have made me in Your image.
You have called me Your child
    and chosen me to be Your servant.
You have assigned to me
    the fantastic responsibility
        of carrying on Your creative activity.

O God,
    how full of wonder and splendor You are!

9

My heart overflows with gratitude to God.
I feel so exuberant,
    I simply must express or explode.
I will give voice to my exaltations;
    I will sing Your praises, O my God.

You helped me stand firm
        despite those who had it in for me,
    and they were not successful
        in their efforts to discredit me.

You have destroyed great forces
        that rose up to oppose You throughout the ages.
You continue to rule over our fractured world,
        to sit in judgment over its nations and peoples.
You offer Your strong hand to those who are oppressed,
        Your loving concern to those who are troubled.
You never hide from those who seek You
        or forsake those who cling to You.

Sing the praises of God;
        proclaim loudly His deeds to the people.
For while He judges evildoers,
        He hears and remembers the cries of those in distress.

I always need Your gracious love.
You know all about my inner fears and doubts.
You hold me back from the brink of destruction.

You make it possible for me to sing Your praises
   and to rejoice in Your perpetual deliverance.
Ungodly nations sink in their own sewage.
Men and women who promote evil
      snare themselves in their own nets,
   but those who recognize their need of You
      shall be found by You.

Is it any wonder
   my heart overflows with gratitude to God?

10

Where in the world are You hiding, O God?
Why are You not available when things go wrong?

The sensualist lives by the desires of the flesh.
The materialist seeks temporal security alone.
The ungodly person indulges in self-worship
      and assumes that God is dead.

The point is, these are the ones who seem to prosper.
They laugh in scorn at those inclined toward piety.
They claim that they are in the driver's seat
      and cannot be dethroned.
They live and speak arrogantly and carelessly.
They lack concern for the enslaved and the deprived.
They take what they want
      without thought for the hurt they cause others.

Wake up, O God! Come out of hiding!
How can You allow these God-defiers to get away with it?

O God, You do take note of those in conflict.
You will take account of the godless and the arrogant.
You are still Lord over all the world.
You do hear the cries of those who love You;
      You are continuously concerned about their needs.
You will enable them to stand up
      against the oppression and pain of this life.

11

I am frightened by the insecurities around me.
I am sorely tempted to run for my life,
　　to take refuge in foolish escapades
　　　　that dim the vision and drug the soul.

There is no escape
　　from the realities of this fractured world.
When we awaken from our stupor
　　　　or return to sobriety,
　　they are ever present
　　　　to haunt and oppress us.

But there is a place of refuge.
God is in our midst.
He is aware of the fears and apprehensions
　　of His beloved children.
He may not always rid us of our fears.
But He does promise to face them with us,
　　to make them stepping-stones to faith,
　　　　to use them to draw us closer to Himself.

I need not worry too much
　　about the distortions of this world.
I do need to be aware that God is here
　　and trust that, through me,
　　　　He will reveal Himself to His world.

12

O God, help me.
The world is truly going to the dogs.
Infidelity and deceit surround me.
Every person seems to wear two faces.

And people even boast about their deeds of evil.
They assume that they can talk themselves
    out of any corner.
They defy authority and live for themselves alone.

Our God will not remain silent forever.
His voice like thunder will drown out
        the foolish boasts of His unfaithful creatures.
"The maligned and the deprived
    have suffered long enough," He will say.
"I will rise to their defense
    and grant them My protection."
And what God promises, He will do.

Keep us, great God, from the indecision and
    vile compromises of this
        valueless generation.

13

O God, sometimes You seem so far away.
I cannot in this moment sense Your presence
   or feel Your power.

The darkness enveloping me is stifling.
This depression is suffocating.
How long, O God, do I have to live in this void?
O God, how long?

Break into this black night, O God;
   fill in this vast emptiness.
Enter into my conflict
   lest I fall, never to rise again.

I continue to trust in Your ever-present love.
I shall again discover true joy
   in my relationship with You.
I will proclaim Your praises, my Lord,
   for You will never let me go.

14

How foolish it is to deny the existence of God
     or to say that God is dead!
And yet many do so.
They say it in the way they live
     if not in the words they speak.

Our great God is forever searching for those
     who live their lives for Him.
He is not looking for
     verbal professions alone
          but active, living testimonies of faith.

He sees denial and rebellion in the lives of all people.
What good they do is tainted by sin and self-centeredness.
They are more apt to be destructive than creative.
How foolish they are
     to neglect God!

It is obvious that God works
     through those who trust Him,
     through those who dedicate their lives
          to His service.
It is they who are set free from self-glory
     to enjoy and to serve the living God.
They truly celebrate the eternal presence of God.

15

Who is the one, O Lord, that demonstrates
   participation in Your kingdom?
What are the prerequisites
   for membership in Your family?

Your child, O Lord, walks cautiously—
   and in obedience to Your precepts and principles.
He is open and honest before God and people.
She speaks and acts in love toward her neighbor.
He cannot condone that which is evil
   and doesn't participate
      in that which promotes injustice.
She listens to her sister's griefs
   and complaints.
He seeks to lighten his brother's burden
   and to share in his sorrow and pain.
She reaches out to heal rather than to hurt,
   to be kind and gentle to all who cross her path.

Those who demonstrate this loving relationship
   with God and His human creatures
   manifest participation in His kingdom.
They will never be separated from the family of God.

16

Sustain me, O God,
   for my faith is anchored in You.
I say it again,
      "You are my Lord;
      when I am estranged from You,
      I have nothing that is of any real worth."

The significant and contributive people
      of this world know You.
I must respect these individuals.
Those who make lesser things their ultimate concern
      are investing in eventual trouble and grief.
I cannot worship their idols
      or respect their objectives.

God has become my ultimate concern.
He is the Pilot of my ship.
Thus the course before me will lead
      to ultimate fulfillment.
I am guaranteed an inheritance of infinite value.

I look to God as my chief counselor.
Even in the darkest night,
      He is ready to teach and guide me.
Because He continually surrounds me,
      I shall not lose my way.

Is it any wonder that I am happy?

Even my humanity, my tangible body,
    rests in the blessed realization of this security.
God will keep even my human self
    from the destructive clutch of evil.

You do show me the paths I must take, O Lord.
Within Your all-embracing presence
    lies genuine fulfillment.
In my relationship with You,
    I discover incomparable and eternal joy.

17

I cry to You out of desperation, my God.
Listen to me and judge me if I am in error.

I have honestly tried to do Your will,
    to promote Your causes, to speak Your Word.
I have avoided the pitfalls that have victimized
    so many around me.
I have acted in love rather than in anger.
I have never raised my hand in violence.
I have walked in the paths You have set before me.

And yet despair trips me up.
There are great walls that I cannot break through,
    dead ends that lead nowhere,
        people to whom I cannot relate.
I reach out in concern and am rebuked with scorn.

I am weary, Lord, weary of well-doing.
I am tired of the reactions
    of those I seek to serve.
I seriously wonder if it is all worth it.

Grant me, O God, a measure of heavenly joy.
Help me feel good about myself
    and about my role in Your service.
Reveal Yourself in some special way this night
    that I may rest in joy and peace.

18

It is no wonder that I love You, O God.
You have granted me a security
　　that I could never find
　　　among the things of this world.

You have erased from my life the fear of death.
What follows the grave no longer causes fearful concern.
The traumatic experiences of this life
　　cannot destroy me.
You are never out of reach
　　but are ever aware of my problems and conflicts.

How great and all-powerful is my God!
　　　The quaking of the earth,
　　　the shaking of the mountains,
　　　the blackness of the night,
　　　the beauty of the heavens,
　　　the lightning that crisscrosses the skies,
　　　the oceans that lash against the shores,
　　　this and much more bears witness
　　　　to the majesty of my God.
And this is the God who is concerned about me.
He reaches into my distraught life
　　to heal my wounds.
He encompasses me with eternal love.
He abides with me
　　even in the midst of conflict or calamity.
He sets me free from self-idolatry
　　so I may serve His creatures around me.

He shields me from the forces that are intent
    on my destruction.
It is no wonder, O God, that I love You.

Can there be any God but this God that I love?
He surrounds me with His strength
    and clothes me with His grace.
He puts into my hands gifts to relay to others.
He entrusts me with tasks
    far beyond my human abilities
    and enables me to carry them out.
He ordains me as His child and servant
    destined to accomplish His purposes
        among the peoples of this world.

Thus I celebrate God's presence
    in my life and world.
God is not dead; He lives!
I rejoice in His concern and love for me.
I will proclaim, O Lord,
    Your praises to anyone who will listen.
I will sing and shout and dance
    in the joy of knowing that You are my God.

19

Wherever I am, wherever I go,
I can sense something of the power of God.
The grandeur of the mountains,
the vastness of the oceans,
the breathtaking wonder of interstellar space;
all this proclaims the glory and majesty of God.
Even amid the clutter of our cities,
built and abused by our hands,
there are reflections of divine splendor.
God's voice can be heard.
He makes His presence known throughout the world.

God has made a path on which we are to walk.
In His will there is order and purpose.
He has proclaimed and demonstrated eternal truth
through the lips and lives of His children.
There are set before men and women precepts
and principles that direct God's creatures
in the way of peace and joy.
He has given meaning to life,
goals and objectives to this existence.
Therein is the answer to our inner need,
the fulfillment of our deepest longings.
These things are more precious and of greater
value than anything we could ever experience
or even dare to imagine.

This is the course which I must travel.
It is not easy; I make so many mistakes.
Faults and obsessions plague me.
O God, forbid that these should destroy me.
Set me free from their tenacious hold.
Encompass me with Your love and grace
that these things may not stand
between You and me.

O God,
these are the thoughts
that crowd my heart today.
Accept them and respond to them.
Enable me to realize anew
the security and serenity
of Your loving presence in my life.

O my very dear friend.
How much I want to bear your burden,
    to share your trouble!
But I can only pray that God may be
    very close to you in your sorrow
    and keep you and protect you in your conflict.
May He remember that you are His own,
    that you have dedicated your life to Him,
    that your heart's desire is to serve and please Him.
May He reach out to touch you and heal you;
    may He fulfill your crying need in this hour.
And may we soon rejoice together over His deliverance
    and walk together in His service.

I know that God does stand by His own.
Our failures do not stay His loving hand.
He transforms them into victories.
People around us put their trust in science and money,
    but such will fail to solve
        the real problems of our lives.
It is only in the name of God
    that we who fall can find the grace to rise again.

Hear my prayer on behalf of my friend, O God.
I want to share in my friend's pain and defeat;
    may I also share in my friend's joy and victory.

21

O God,
   in the grace and strength that You grant daily,
      Your servant finds reason for celebration.
You have truly fulfilled my innermost longings.
You have responded to my deepest needs.

I asked for security,
   and You encompassed me with love.
I looked to You for life,
   and You granted me life everlasting.
I sought for identity,
   and You adopted me as Your child.
Whatever is of value and worth in my life
   has come through Your rich blessings.
My heart is glad in the realization
   of Your eternal presence.
I know that I will never lose Your love.

I raise my voice in praise, O God,
   because no one can separate me from You.
Though circumstances threaten me
      and my own obsessions entangle me,
   You will never let me go.
Your great power is sufficient to set me free
   from these things that hurt my soul.
I put my trust in You;
   You will not let them destroy me.
I find so many reasons for praising You, O God.

O God, why have You left me?
Why are You so far from me?
I can no longer feel You near.
I reach desperately for You,
    but I cannot find You.

I know You are holy and all-righteous
    and everywhere present.
The saints of past years believed in You
    and trusted You.
You responded to their cries.
They sought You, and they found You.
It is no wonder that Your praises
    were constantly on their lips.

But I feel as empty and insignificant
    as a bag full of wind.
I don't really expect people's plaudits,
    but I so sorely feel their criticisms.
I risk all in following
    what I feel to be Your will for me;
        yet even my friends fail to support me,
        and they actually turn against me.
"He thinks he's doing God's will," they say.
"But he'll be sorry he made that decision."

I believe that You have been with me
    from the very beginning of my life.

I know that You have cared for me
    through these many years.
But, God, I need You now.
I am in trouble,
    and I can't find You or feel You near.
At this moment, I feel as if I am falling apart.
Nothing seems to make sense anymore.
Everything I attempt ends in failure.
I feel inferior and weak.
Those I have tried to serve
    are actually gloating
        over my flops and failures.
I know, O God, that much of it
    is a matter of my foolish feelings.
The fact is, You are not far off.
You know both my feelings and my failings.
Yet You love me and accept me.
You will save me—even from myself.

Thus I will continue to sing Your praises.
In spite of or in scorn of my feelings,
    I will celebrate Your loving presence.
As despicable as I may feel at times,
    You do not despise me. Neither will You leave me.
Your love is personal, and it is eternal.

Nor will You despise or ignore the afflictions
    that plague Your many sons and daughters.

Your children and servants are precious to You.
Even when they fail You, You never fail them.
You hear their cries and feel their pain
    and are ever ready to support them
        in their conflicts.

I dedicate myself anew to You, O Lord.
I will serve You
    whatever the cost or the consequence.
You are my God.
Regardless of my feelings
    of insignificance and inadequacy,
I will praise Your name and proclaim Your love
    to people all around me.

23

The Lord is my constant companion.
There is no need that He cannot fulfill.
Whether His course for me points
          to the mountaintops of glorious joy
          or to the valleys of human suffering,
     He is by my side.
     He is ever present with me.
He is close beside me
     when I tread the dark streets of danger,
     and even when I flirt with death itself,
     He will not leave me.
When the pain is severe,
     He is near to comfort.
When the burden is heavy,
     He is there to lean upon.
When depression darkens my soul,
     He touches me with eternal joy.
When I feel empty and alone,
     He fills the aching vacuum with His power.
My security is in His promise
          to be near me always
     and in the knowledge
          that He will never let me go.

24

Let us never forget that this world
　　and everything in it belongs to God.
But not all of this world's citizens
　　recognize or give allegiance to their Creator.

Who are the ones who truly love and serve God?
They are the people who discover and live
　　within His purposes for their lives.
They are the people whose hearts and hands
　　are dedicated to His will for them.
They are the people who turn away from
　　　self-centered concerns
　　to live for those around them.
They can count on God's perpetual blessings.
They have been delivered from anxiety
　　to focus their efforts on communicating
　　　God's eternal love to people around them.

Let us look up and live!
God is present in all His glory and majesty.
Let us let go and celebrate!
Our loving Lord is here with us
　　and will manifest Himself through us.
We represent Him in all His saving power.
We are His beloved and empowered servants
　　in this world that He created.

25

I am reaching for You again, O God.
From the abyss of defeat,
    the suffocating shame of failure,
        I seek Your mercy and Your help.
Enable me to see Your will for my life.
Break through this stifling darkness
    with some direction, some meaning,
        some purpose for my existence.
You are my God; You have promised me salvation.
How long must I wait for Your response?

Have You given up on me, O Lord?
Are You remembering the uncountable times
    that I have failed You?
Then I am remembering Your steadfast love,
    Your concern for those
        who fail and fumble,
    Your efforts to restore those
        who humbly reach out for You.
I know well that those
    who walk in Your course for their lives
        find contentment and fulfillment.
I have tried to do so, and again I have failed.
I am aware that those who serve You
    will know true security and abundance.
I have sought this only to be snared
    and incapacitated by my own weaknesses.

O God, have mercy!
I know my guilt is great.
Look upon my emptiness and loneliness,
    consider kindly my afflictions and despair,
    remember the perpetual presence
      of my human weaknesses and instincts.
Regard once more the pernicious and violent forces
    that oppose Your will in my life.
Forgive me my many sins,
    and restore me to Yourself.
Watch over me and hold on to me, O God,
    lest I fall again.

26

I am about to make an important decision, Lord,
   and the day before me is charged with uncertainty.
Enable me to sense Your presence,
   to feel Your strengthening power,
   to be assured of Your guiding concern.

I have been Your child and servant for many years.
Even in my youth I claimed Your redeeming love
   and dedicated my life to Your purposes.
Until now I have shunned the world's enticements,
   the human ambitions that so teasingly beckon,
   to pursue Your objectives
      and carry out Your commands.

I have been faithful to the hour of worship
   and the time of prayer.
I have celebrated Your grace and sung Your praises.
My dearest friends are those who love and serve You.

Now, O Lord, I have come to a fork in the road.
I don't know which way to turn.
I commit this day into Your hands.
I pray that it may be lived by Your direction
   and in accord with Your will.

I raise my voice in thanksgiving, O God,
   for You have granted me the assurance
      that You will guide my faltering steps.

With the living and eternal God as my goal and guide,
 fear and anxiety need have no place in my life.
All the evil in the world cannot destroy Him
 nor can it destroy anyone within His loving embrace.
The very legions of hell lay siege to my soul,
 only to be thwarted by a power far greater.

I have one primary and ultimate desire:
 to abide within the love and acceptance of God.
Within His tender care I know I am safe.

Thus I shall stand tall
 regardless of threatening enemies
  and the tyranny of evil.
I will counter the subtle voices of temptation
 with exclamations of praise to my God.

My God does hear when I cry out to Him.
He does not ignore my needs;
 neither is He indifferent to my desires.
He will not let me go even if my own family
 should turn against me.
He will sustain me and keep me on course
 through the dangers and pitfalls of this life.

It is possible to know and experience God's love
 in this uncertain, tumultuous existence.
Take courage, step out in faith, scorn the consequences,
 and let God have His way with you.

28

O God, I am crying for help!
This is not a pious exclamation—
    I mean it! I'm desperate!
If You don't listen, I'll go down the drain!

Don't let me float downstream
    with those who ignore You.
I know they will go over the edge if they persist
    in their course of rebelliousness and indifference.
Reach out, O God,
    and snatch me from this overpowering current
        lest I perish with them.

I thank You, O God.
You have heard my agonizing cry.
I called for You, and You responded.
You are my Hope and my Salvation.
I will sing Your praises forever.

And thus the Lord is the Hope and Salvation
    of all who trust in Him.
Stay close to those who struggle, O God,
    never let them go.

29

We need to give credit to whom credit is due.
God is alive,
    and He deserves our perpetual praises.
There is reason for rejoicing.
There is a God to worship and love.

The skies and the forests
    manifest His beauty.
The sweep of the ocean
    represents His power.
The gigantic bodies suspended in
    our universe portray His majesty.
The wind and the rain,
    the lightning and the thunder,
    the creatures that inhabit the land,
    the flowers that brighten our lives,
        all this comes from the hand of God.
The glory is not ours but God's.

Even the achievements
    of human hand, mind, and machine
    come through the wisdom and power
        of the eternal God.
The contributions of science;
    the fields ripe for harvest;
    the control of water, air, and space;
    the establishment of our great institutions—
        these also reflect the glory of God.

Let us give credit to whom credit is due.
Let us rejoice in the God who blesses us.
Let us seek His grace to serve Him
  by serving others with the abundance
  that He bestows upon us.

30

In a world where there are people
who assume You no longer exist,
I am compelled to proclaim Your praises, O God.
I cannot define or describe You,
but I know from personal experience
Your power and presence in my life.
There was a time when I screamed,
"Good Lord, where are You?"
Then You touched my despairing soul with healing
and delivered me from my private little hell.
Thus I shout Your praises, O my God,
and exhort all who know You to do the same.
There are times when I feel Your anger,
but even then I know
Your concern and love for me remain eternal.
Then my nights of despair
resolve into the dawn of new joy.

There was a time when I thought I was secure
among my material accumulations.
However, they gathered like a cloud
to blot out the face of God,
and I was left empty and unfulfilled.

I finally came to my senses
and returned to You, O God.
"Lord," I said, "my well-deserved damnation
would also be a loss to You.

I cannot praise You from the pits of hell
   or proclaim Your loving-kindness
      from the grave of eternal death.
So have mercy, Lord,
   and help me out of this dark fog."

And You turned my griping into gratitude,
   my screams of despair into proclamations of joy.
Now I can explode with praises,
   and I will spend eternity in thanksgiving to You.

31

I am up a blind alley, Lord.
The props have been knocked out from beneath me.
I feel as if I'm grappling with the wind
    for some support or security.
I've been pulled up short, Lord.
Now I realize how much I need
    something or someone
    beyond and above myself
        to give stability to my tenuous existence.
Maybe it was Your doing, Lord.
Maybe You are bringing me back to home port,
    correcting my focus
        and reassessing my goals.

I return to You with empty hands, Lord.
You know well my sorry plight.
I did not find that secret treasure,
    that pearl of great price.
The bright lights that beckoned
    only led me astray.
I became entangled in the bonds of self-service.
Everything I touched turned to dust in my hands.

I despise myself today, Lord.
Even those I thought were my friends
    turn their faces from me.
There is no place to go, nothing to cling to.
I can only come back to You
    and cast myself on Your loving mercy.

You are my God.
You never let me out of Your sight.
Even when I strike out on my own,
    You pursue me and hold on to me.

I've stopped running, Lord.
From this point on
    I will place my hours and days
        into Your loving hands.
I seek only Your guidance
    and the grace and strength
        to carry out Your purposes.
Restore me, O God,
    to Your program and design for my life.

Thank You for taking me back, Lord,
    for renewing my relationship with You.
I seek now to walk in Your course for me.
I shall abide forever in Your steadfast love.
I will proclaim Your praises
    and live out Your purposes.
Enable me to be faithful to You,
        whatever the consequences,
    and to celebrate Your love
        and to communicate it to everyone around me.

32

The person who knows the meaning of forgiveness,
     who is no longer plagued by past failures,
     who stands blameless and guilt-free before God,
         that person is rich indeed.

Every time I attempt to handle my own guilt—
     by ignoring it, rationalizing it,
     or just running away from it—
     some unseen power or pressure
         from the depths of my being
     squeezes my life dry, leaving me empty.

But when I face up to my failures and confess them,
     when I open my guilt-ridden heart
         to You, O God,
     then I realize the blessed meaning
         of forgiveness.

Thus everyone who claims faith in the loving God
     needs to cling to His acceptance and concern.
Times of darkness will come.
     Life's storms and tempests will continue to rage,
         but the faithful shall not be destroyed.

You are, O God, a place of refuge.
     You enable us to face our problems,
     You keep us from being destroyed by them.

Even within the darkness surrounding me,
    in the midst of life's turmoil,
    I can hear the voice of God:
"Even these things serve a purpose in your life.
Don't sell them short
    for they are steps along My path for you.
Stop being stubborn and stupid
    like some undiscerning jackass
        that has to be driven with sticks or whips."

The faithful and the faithless both suffer
    the uncertainties and insecurities of this life,
    but the children of God can depend always
        on the love of their Father.
It is for this reason that there is
    light even in the midst of darkness,
    incomprehensible joy in the midst of sorrow,
    and we can find a measure of happiness
        and well-being
        regardless of the circumstances that surround us.

33

God is here—let's celebrate!
With song and with dance,
    with stringed instruments and brass,
    with cymbals and drums,
let us express exuberant joy in God's presence.
Let us celebrate with the old songs of praise.
Let us also create new songs
    that portray the eternal love of our God.

He did create this world.
He continues to permeate it with His love.
Even among its frustrated and unbelieving children,
    He constantly carries out His purposes.
His plans for His world and its inhabitants
    are not obliterated by the foolishness
        of men and women.
His truth is not blotted out by the lethargy or lies
    of His apathetic creatures.
He continues to reign and to reveal Himself to us.

And God continues to create and to renew
    the world around us.
He does this through those who are His own,
    who rely on His ever-present love.
He delivers His children from the fear of death
    and through them gives life to this world.
God's love is sure and everlasting.
Hearts open to His love are filled with joy.
They truly find cause for celebration.

34

I feel as if I could never cease praising God.
Come and rejoice with me over His goodness!

I reached for Him out of my inner conflicts,
    and He was there
        to give me strength and courage.
I wept in utter frustration over my troubles,
    and He was near to help and support me.

What He has done for me He can do for you.
Turn to Him; He will not turn away from you.
His loving presence
    encompasses those who yield to Him.
He is with them
    in the midst of their troubles and conflicts.
He meets their emptiness with His abundance
    and shores up their weakness
        through His divine power.

Listen to me; I know whereof I speak.
I have learned through experience
    that this is the way to happiness.
God is ever alert to the cries of His children;
    He feels and bears with them
        their pains and problems.

He is near to those who suffer
and reaches out to help
those who are battered down by despair.
Even the children of God experience affliction,
but they have a loving Father
who will keep them and watch over them.

The godless suffer in loneliness, without hope;
the servants of God find meaning and purpose
even in the midst of suffering and conflict.

35

It is not easy, Lord, to follow after You.
While You take the hard road
    with joyous leaps and bounds,
   I stumble over every stone
    and slip into every rut.
You calmly weather each storm
    and walk fearlessly through the night.
I am buffeted by the winds,
    and I falter in the darkness.

And You always have answers, Lord,
    for those who confront You.
My tongue is thick and clumsy.
I cannot articulate what I believe
    or what they need to hear.
You have the wisdom and the power
    to meet the needs of people around You.
But I am foolish and ineffective,
    and my sisters and brothers turn away
      from me in disgust.

I have really tried to relate to people around me,
    to reach out in love and concern.
I have shared their sorrows and their joys.
I have shelved my ambitions
    to respond to their needs.

But when I fail to produce what they want,
    or when I am limited by my humanity
        and incapacitated by my personal problems,
        they will have nothing to do with me.
I feel as if I have been used only to be abused.
I am squeezed dry and then cast aside.

Yet I must continue to follow You, O Lord.
It is a hard path to walk,
    and I will falter at times.
I long intensely for an occasional oasis
    along this journey through wind and sand.
I need desperately Your touch of joy and enrichment
    as I labor amid the blood and tears
        of this distorted world.
I am empty, Lord,
    enable me to sense Your fullness
    and grant to me the grace and the courage
        to be faithful as Your child and servant.

36

It amazes me how some people can be so self-centered,
    so indifferent and calloused
        to the desires and needs of others.
Not only do they neglect God;
    they are totally oblivious of Him
        and have no fear of Him.
And then they convince themselves that this is life,
    that the world spins around them
        and they must satiate their own desires
            regardless of the hurt it causes others.

And yet Your all-pervading love, O God,
    which extends far beyond
        the dimensions of our conscious lives,
    includes even these distorted people
        who spurn You in exchange for
            twisted, self-centered lives.

Your eternal love is beyond comprehension.
No wonder Your children constantly reach for it
    and find security within it.
Within that love, O Lord, You answer our needs
    and fulfill our desires.

Continue to pour out Your saving love
    upon those who follow You.
Do not allow the arrogance and infidelity of the godless
    to deter us from Your course for our lives.

37

It's high time we stop complaining
about the corruption of our world
or the lack of values in our society.
It seems like at the same time we complain,
we eye with envy those ungodly characters
who appear to have more fun
or to be more successful than we are.

If we really trusted in God
and were truly committed to His purposes,
the world might be better off today.
God is in our world.
He is the source
of our joy and well-being,
the fulfillment of our hearts' desires.
God works through those who are dedicated
to Him and His will
to permeate this world's darkness
with divine light.

Let's stay calm and try to be patient.
Stop worrying
about the apparent hopelessness of it all.
We only contribute to this despair
with our negativity and defeatism.
God has not taken a vacation; He is here.

He has His own way of dealing
    with corruption and greed,
    disease and bigotry,
    war and violence,
    insecurity and fear.

The ultimate victory is God's.
Those who live within God's will
    shall surely discover
      that His purposes prevail,
      that true joy and peace and security
        come from Him.

Let us wait on God and seek daily to obey Him.
He is our salvation and our security,
    and nothing in this world
      can take that away from us.
Ask Him to calm our hostilities,
    to overcome our anxieties,
      and to help us walk in peace and love.

38

O God, how angry You must be with me!
I feel as if I were
   pierced through with a red-hot iron,
   stifled with the heavy hand of judgment.

I am falling apart.
I am sick to death with sin and failure,
   broken and spent, wretched and miserable,
   flat on my face in despair.

Even those I once called my friends
      now keep their distance
   while others actually gloat over my predicament.
But I am becoming numb
   to their glances of suspicion or pity
   and their self-righteous rebukes.
I have ceased trying to defend myself
   or respond to their accusations.
I've had it; I am ready to throw in the towel.
   I simply cannot take it any longer.

You are aware of my anguish, my God.
You feel my misery.
I know that I have grieved You,
   and I am truly sorry for my sin.
Don't turn away from me, O God.
   Don't leave me in this abominable mess.
Save me now, O God, lest I be damned forever.

39

I said to myself, "I'll watch it—
    I'll grit my teeth and hold in my anger
        at least as long as I am
        among ungodly people."

And I honestly tried, but it was no use.
The pressures increased.
The more I stewed about it,
        the more frustrated I became.

Finally I exploded:
"O God, demonstrate some concern for me.
Give me some reason for this endless conflict,
        some objective for this fast-ebbing life of mine.
You made me what I am,
        and the span of my existence
        is but a speck of dust to You.
This is true about every human being.
A person is no more than a smidgen of moist air
        or a shadow without lasting substance.
Men and women endure this temporal turmoil
        for no reason whatsoever.
They agonize and toil
        only to leave the fruits for someone else to enjoy.

"So I wonder what in the world it's all about.
I have no hope at all except in You.
I continue to lay claim
        to Your forgiveness for my failures.

Keep me from being
  despised and abhorred
    by my fellow creatures.
Lift Your heavy hand from me;
    I am utterly weary of its oppressing weight.
When You punish people with judgment of their failures,
    You suck up like a tornado
      everything that is precious to them.
Surely they are no more than a passing cloud
    on the eternal horizon.

"Hear and decipher these confusing thoughts of mine.
    Lend Your ear to these agonizing cries.
      Do not turn away from my pains and problems.
I am just a swiftly passing traveler,
    as were all who have gone before me.
Let me have just a morsel of happiness
    before I leave this world
      and enter into oblivion."

40

I searched long and shouted loud for God.
It finally paid off. He responded.
He reached into my pathetic emptiness
    and planted objective and purpose.
Now I feel like singing;
    there is genuine meaning in my life.
And I can tell others about the
    prominent place God holds in my heart.
Those who are thoroughly fed up
        with the fly-by-night objectives
            of this ephemeral existence,
    who will look to their Creator
        and seek out His will for them,
        they also will find something to sing about.
There is love and concern in Him,
    and meaning and purpose,
        far more than one can possibly imagine.

Our God is not looking for genius;
    He does not require great talent.
He is not charmed by our panic-ridden activity.
He simply asks for our faith and our obedience.
It was when He turned me from self-seeking
    to follow His will for my life
        that I discovered serenity and security.

Thus I am compelled to express in word and in deed
    the glad news of God's love and concern
        to anyone who will listen.
And the Lord knows
    that I have honestly tried to do this.
My frailties and my failures are many,
    but I have not cheated on this score.
I have proclaimed the salvation
    that God offers to all.

But my conflicts have not ceased.
My sin-permeated nature still plagues me.
I still feel overwhelmed at times
    by my faults and fallibilities.
I am disturbed and depressed
    when others fail to understand or accept me.
I need to rely on the grace of God.

God grant that all who search for life's meaning
    may discover it
        in a relationship of love and trust with Him.
Then they shall know His greatness
    and proclaim His praises.
As for me, foolish and sinful though I am,
    I know that God will never cease to love me.

41

I believe that people who give of themselves
    for the sake of others,
  who demonstrate genuine concern
    for those who are less fortunate,
  are especially blessed by God.
They are precious in God's eyes
    and are protected by Him.
Even as they face the hatred of their enemies
      or the conflicts and illnesses of this existence,
    the Lord delivers and sustains them.

It is for this reason that I dare to claim
    God's gracious intervention on my behalf.
It is true that my sins are many.
I reach desperately for God's forgiving mercy.
I receive no comfort from many
    who I thought were my friends.
I could drop dead; they couldn't care less.
When we meet,
    their words are empty,
    their thoughts pregnant with suspicion.
When we part,
    they go out to spread their suspicions abroad,
      imagining the worst about me
        and whispering behind my back.

I can imagine their conversation:
   "One would think she'd be
     beyond this sort of thing.
   Why she's as bad as the worst of them.
   She's had it! She won't crawl out of this!"
Even the one person I trusted the most,
     in whom I confided,
   with whom I lovingly related,
   even she looks down her nose at me
     as one she would rather step on than support.
She no longer wants anything to do with me.

My loving God, You are truly gracious to me.
You have not cast me aside
   or allowed me to be destroyed.
You know that I honestly want to serve You.
And You have demonstrated
   Your acceptance and concern for me
     by sustaining me
     and drawing me even closer to Yourself.
May God be praised forever!

42

As a desert wanderer longs for springs of cool water,
so my thirsty soul reaches out for You, O God.
How I long for a deeper sense of Your presence,
for a faith that will embrace You
without fear or doubt!
Yet while I weep in longing, people around me say,
"If God is not dead, where is He?"

I remember so well the faith of my childhood.
How real God was to me in those days
when I prayed and sang praises
and listened to His Word
in the fellowship of family and friends!
Then why am I so depressed now?
Why can't I recapture the joy and confidence
of those years?
I remember the stories of Your love
that I was taught;
how merciful and all-powerful were Your dealings
with Your children throughout history!
Yet now my heart is empty,
and waves of doubt flood over my soul.

I pray, but the heavens, too, are empty.
It is almost as if God has forgotten all about me.
And while I struggle with the sickness of doubt,
people around me say,
"If God is not dead, where is He?"

O foolish heart, why do you seethe in unrest?
God has not changed;
 His love for me is ever the same.
He will renew my faith in Him;
 I can again shout His praises
  even when I don't feel His presence.
Truly He is God,
 and He is my Help and my Hope.

O God,
  my life is cluttered with conflicts.
And there are times
  when You seem oblivious to it all.
The pitfalls before me, the weaknesses within me—
  all this is most depressing.
I feel as if I am groping in utter darkness.

Break into my darkness, O God.
Set me free from my hang-ups.
May the daily pressures
    that threaten to strangle me
  drive me to Your fountainhead of grace.
Then night will give way to dawn,
    depression shall resolve into joy,
      and I shall sing Your praises once more.

O foolish spirit,
  why do you fret over so many things?
God is here!
He knows all about your troubles and trials.
Renew your faith in Him and rejoice.

I shall rejoice!
No matter how dark the night,
  God is my ever-present and eternal Hope.

O God,
    I have heard so much about how close You were
        to Your children throughout history.
They conquered the enemy
        and credited You for their victories.
When they were defeated,
    they accepted their lot
        as Your righteous judgment.
They assumed they were Your beloved charges
        and accepted their afflictions
        as from Your hand.
Their persistent faith in You
    held them together
        through the crises of their lives.

And I am aware of how You have watched over me
    in the midst of my conflicts.
You have enabled me to overcome
    the obstacles in my life.
Even when I failed miserably,
    You set me on my feet again
        and directed me on Your course for my life.
I am keenly aware of my incapabilities
    and inadequacies
        and of how much I need You.
I know all this, Lord.
You have been an integral part
    of my life's experiences.
I am deeply grateful for Your care and concern.

But what about today, O Lord?
I am on the spot—and I can't reach You.

It seems as if You have left the scene,
    and I am left holding the bag.
I cry for help
    and hear only the echo of my own voice.
I grope around me
    and find insurmountable walls and dark corners.
The advice of my peers and superiors
    seems devoid of genuine love or concern.
O God, if You are truly my God,
    reveal Yourself to me now.
I simply cannot bear the shame and the pain
    of my problem.
Nobody around me can help me.
If people knew about it,
    they would only shun me.

I have not forgotten You, O God.
I do believe in You as I have been taught.
I worshiped You and sang Your praises
    when all was well.
I have dedicated my life to You and Your purposes.
Now I am in deep trouble.
I have no one else to turn to.

O God, listen to me.
Respond to my cry for help.
Deliver me from this terrible conflict
    before it destroys me.
Help me sense Your loving concern.
Save me before it is too late.

45

My heart is full of joy today.
I reach almost frantically for the sounds
    that might express that joy,
    the words that would proclaim the exuberance
    that I feel at this moment.
I am overwhelmed with praise,
    and I must express it lest I succumb to it.

You, my dear friend, were the source of this joy.
You touched me with love
    and awakened my sleeping heart
        to the beauty and fragrance of life around me.
God reached out through your devotion and concern
    to kindle anew a fire within me,
        to fan embers into flames of light and faith.
You marched into my jungle of despair
    and made a path for me to walk on once more.
You sliced through my confusion
    and gave order and motivation
        to my purposeless gropings.

I am so very grateful—to God and to you.
I pray that God may use me,
        as He has so abundantly used you,
    to transmit joy to the joyless,
        despairing lives of those who cross my path.
And I pray that God may bless you
    and keep you and use you forever.

46

Our great God is still our Refuge and Strength.
     He knows our problems and fears.
Thus we have no business doubting Him
          even though the earth is convulsed in tragedy
               or its human masses threatened
                    by ethnic hatred, disease,
                    drugs, crime, or abuse.

God continues to reign as all-wise
          and as almighty as ever.
His eternal plan is not canceled out
          by the whims of human leaders
               or the freakish accidents of nature.
Nations will destroy each other.
          Civilizations will perish.
          The earth itself may one day become
               a smoking cinder, but God will not leave us.
He is forever our sure Refuge and Strength.

Just look around you; read the pages of history.
Refresh your flagging spirit with the reminder
          of His great feats throughout the ages.
And you will again hear Him speaking:
          "Relax, stop fretting, and
               remember that I am still your God.
          I still hold the reins of this world."

God is here among us.
          He continues to be our Refuge and Strength.

47

Clap your hands! Stomp your feet!
Let your bodies and your voices
        explode with joy.
God is not some human concoction.
He is for real! And He is here!
Despite all attempts
        to rationalize Him out of existence,
    God is in our world,
        and He reigns over our universe.

The rulers of nations often ignore Him.
People of learning often pass Him by.
The masses of His creatures substitute
        their own little gods in His place
        and worship the things they can see and feel.
Others build fortresses around themselves
        and announce no need for God.

Our great God will not be ignored.
He will not remove Himself from our world.
Let us recognize His presence
        and fill the air with His praises.

48

How great is my God!
He soars above our poor intellects
    like a snow-capped mountain
        over a sun-baked desert.
He scatters the profound theories
        of wise men and women
    like leaves pushed around by a winter wind.
He shatters
    the assembled might of world governments
        as an earthquake levels a city.
He reaches down in tenderness
    to earth's poor creatures
  and draws them to Himself.

Consider with me the greatness of my God.
Measure His judgments;
    embrace His eternal love.
Stand tall in your faith,
    courageous in your commitment,
    for He is truly a great God.

49

How foolish are the creatures of God!
They accumulate wealth
    and imagine themselves secure
       in possessions and property.
Or they use some inborn gift
    and bask in the plaudits of their peers.
They live for themselves alone
    and give no thought to eternity.
They claim that God is simply
    not necessary to their existence.
He is just a big thumb in the sky
    designed to pacify the weak and the childish.
They claim that they must be
    sufficient unto themselves.
They don't need the extra baggage
    of faith and religion.

But when riches melt away,
    health fails, talents wear thin,
    and remaining years become few,
    when no one honors them
       or expresses concern,
    then these foolish creatures stand naked and exposed
       in empty despair.
Their fortress is breached;
    they are flattened and defeated.
Life, what little of it there is left,
    no longer has meaning for them.

Then they may look desperately for the God
    they discarded in their youth.

Let us consider carefully the security
    of a loving relationship with God.
Let us mouth His praises
    and demonstrate in our lives the eternal joy
        of knowing Him and living as His children.
We need not depend on this world's wealth
    nor the accolades of human beings.
We need not fear the end of our days
    upon this earth.
God is forever—
    and also the souls of those
        who are committed to Him.

Clap your hands! Shout for joy!
God is real, and He is here!

50

God is indeed in our world.
From dawn to dusk,
from twilight hours to the first light
on the eastern horizon,
God is near us and around us.

God speaks to our world.
He speaks gently in love
and thunders fiercely in judgment.
He calls to those who are faithful to Him.
He comforts them and challenges them.
He secures them and sends them forth.

God is at work in our world.
He works in and through the lives of His children
who are loyal and obedient to Him.
"Don't bring your sacrifices to human altars
or build churches and erect memorials
on My behalf,"
He would say to us today.
"I already own the gifts you bring.
All these things have come to you from My hand.
You are to offer them on the altar of humanity's need.
These are the sacrifices that get through to Me
and are accepted by Me."

It is thus that God touches the lives of needy people.
It is by way of the self-sacrificing love
of His servants.

God judges our world.
This judgment falls upon those
    who live totally for themselves.
They are indifferent to the needs of others.
No matter how impressive their rituals
      and religious exercises,
    their lives do not please God.

God is in our world.
We serve Him with the kind of worship
      and thanksgiving
    that effectively communicates His love
      to His children in need around us.

51

O God, may the measure of Your eternal love
    be the measure of Your mercy.
And may the measure of Your mercy
    be sufficient to blot out my great sins
        and cancel out the guilt of my wrongdoings.

I have failed, O Lord, and my failures
    weigh heavily upon my heart.
I cannot share them all with my brothers or sisters
    lest they weigh too heavily upon them
        or even threaten our relationship.
But You know what they are, O God,
    and how far I have fallen short
        of Your standards and expectations.

I am only human, Lord.
It was not by my choice that I was propelled
    into this fractured world.
The weaknesses that plague me
    are not all my doing
        nor can I handle them by my strength alone.

I know that nothing can be hidden from You.
I can only acknowledge my indictment
    and beg for Your loving forgiveness.
Purge me of my guilt, O Lord.
    Heal the hurts of those
        who have been afflicted by my failures.

Revive my flagging spirit, O God.
Restore to me the joy and assurance
    of a right relationship with You.
Reinstate me in Your purposes,
    and help me avoid
        the snares and pitfalls along this earthly path.

It is only then that my tongue will be set free
        to sing Your praises
    and my hands to perform the tasks
        You have set before me.
It is only then that I can have a
    deep and meaningful relationship
        with my brothers and sisters,
    and communicate to them
        the message of Your reconciling love.

I bring You no oblation or sacrifice, my God,
    only a foolish and self-centered heart.
I come to You with a sincere desire
        to be Your servant,
    to walk in Your course for my life,
    to bask in Your love and reflect it
        to those around me.

I thank You, God, that this is acceptable to You
    and that I will remain Your child forever.

52

There are many clever people
  who apparently have no need for God.
With their keen wits and sharp tongues,
    they seduce their fellow creatures and use them
      to promote their own selfish ambitions.
They barge around this world as if they owned it
    and have no consideration for those
      they hurt in the process.
They brashly step on one another
    in their avid pursuit of riches and power.
They scorn those they brush aside
    and destroy those who stand in their way.
They flaunt their achievements before others
    and brag about their self-sufficiency.
They demean those poor fools
    who support and applaud them
      in their ascent to their worldly thrones.

They will be toppled,
    these ambitious people and their thrones of clay.
From the dust they came;
    to the dust they shall return.
Their cleverness will dissolve into emptiness.
Their boasting will become like a hot wind.
Their achievements shall become as nothing,
    and they shall grovel before the victims
      of their atrocious acts.

This is not so with the children of God.
They may never know earthly success
    and may never be inundated with temporal riches,
    but they are eternally secure in the love of God.
Like green trees that spread their boughs
        to shield the weary traveler
    or hold out their fruit to the hungry stranger,
        God's children quietly and continually carry out
        God's purposes in a barren land.

53

Those who proclaim that God is dead
    are veritable fools.
They presume to speak
        as sophisticated intellectuals;
        they are in reality, possibly unconsciously,
            promoting depravity.

God is ever probing the hearts of men and women,
    marking those who seek after Him.

He finds instead
        that great masses of His creatures
        are following after other gods.
And without realizing it,
        they are leading one another
            to certain destruction.
It is no wonder there is such confusion and terror
    in the world.
It is mostly perpetuated
    by those who have no use for God.
O may our great God restore
        the hearts of His foolish creatures
            to Himself.

54

I come in thanksgiving and praise, O God.
Help me articulate the gratitude
that I feel toward You.

I was tripped up by my own pride
and confounded by my own foolishness.
I said things and did things that hurt others
and dishonored You.
I stumbled into a net of my own making
from which I could not escape.

Then You heard my cries and saw my plight.
You touched me with Your love and set me free
to walk with You once more.
You continue to deliver me
from the snares and pitfalls surrounding me.

This is why I rejoice, O God.
It is because of this that I offer myself to You.
May Your ever-present love for me
urge me to demonstrate love toward others
who are troubled and afraid.

I am terribly alone, O God,
   and I don't know where to turn.
I thought I was really living
   when I came to the city—
   set free from the restraints
      of childhood and youth.
But now I am frightened.
The people around me are cold and indifferent.
No one knows that I exist.
The traffic by day and the neon glare
      that pushes back the night
      are strange and unfriendly.
I feel as if I am hopelessly lost
   in some concrete wilderness.
The streets lead nowhere—
   except to blend into other streets.
It's a wilderness filled with violence.
Its creatures are dazed, sick, hungry, or angry.
Oppression, crime, and injustice flourish.
Blood often flows in the streets.
And I can hardly see the blue sky by day
      or the stars by night
   or hear the songs of birds
      or the tolling bells of a church.

It was exciting at first.
I even had a friend with whom I explored
   the mysteries of the city.
Maybe I could have endured
   and found happiness with my friend.

But my friend turned into an enemy
    who no longer needed me
    and melted into the crowds
        that walk down my street.

Then the city became barren and desolate.
The bright lights became ghostly,
    the people around me like zombies
        or puppets on strings,
    the clamor and noise hideous and discordant.
And now my soul has become as bleak
    as the city.

I am lonely, O God, but I am not alone.
You are here in the city.
O God, lead me to You.
Enable me, my God,
    to serve You here in the city.

O God, I have tried diligently
   to reflect Your love to people around me.
I shared my possessions;
   I gave of my time;
   I used Your gifts to me to support,
      to help, and to bless others
         who were in need.

But I feel as if I have been used, O God.
People have wiped their feet on me.
They take what I offer and then go their own way,
   totally oblivious to my problems and pains.
They act as if I were in debt to them—
   as if it were my duty to share myself with them.

But even as I groan in complaint, O Lord,
   I know that this is Your course for me.
Even as they use You, so they will use me.
Truly, O God, I have nothing to lose,
   for it is in losing that I truly find
      that which is of everlasting value.

You are aware of my frustrations,
   my feelings of emptiness and loneliness.
You have promised to replenish me
   and use me to channel Your eternal springs
   to those suffering around me.

I am emptied again and again—
only to be filled from Your boundless resources.
Through me Your blessings are poured out
upon those in need.

You have delivered me from the wasteland.
Therefore I dedicate myself anew
to the task of sharing Your gifts
with those still treading a parched path.

Encompass me with Your love and mercy,
gracious Lord;
I have no security except in You.
I am continually exposed
to the destructive forces of this existence.
I am in constant danger of losing the battle
to the passions and desires
of my own nature.
I can only submit myself to You
and trust that You will fulfill
Your purposes in me.

Your love, O God, is steadfast;
Your grace is everlasting.

Even when I am beaten down by depression,
ensnared by my weaknesses and frailties,
and even when my own lust threatens to devour me,
You are my God,
and You will not let me go.

I am determined to serve You, O Lord.
May my life be a continual thankoffering to You.
I shall sing Your praises forever.

58

My heart grieves, O Lord,
  for the leaders of this world
    who play god with the lives of men and women.
With the clever twisting of half-truths
  they gather followers into their folds
    and manipulate them
    into carrying out their purposes.
They blind people to personal conscience
    and responsibility
  and enslave them to their immoral wishes
    and sinful ambitions.

Then there are velvet-voiced mystics who assume
    they are God's special gift to humankind
  and who,
    through devious tricks or inscrutable gifts,
    create their cults of loyal disciples.

You shall have the last word, O God,
  and those who take Your place,
    or who stand in Your way
    as You seek to draw people to Yourself,
  will be subjected to Your judgments.

You are my God, Almighty and Eternal.
Forbid, O God, that I should ever turn from You
  to follow the false shepherds of this world.

59

Deliver me, O God, from the enemies of my soul.
I am no longer afraid of people who stand in my way,
        even those who obstruct Your purposes
            or who deceive their fellow beings
                with their arrogant and clever clichés.
They anger me, but they do not frighten me.
My pain and confusion come because
        of my own weaknesses and faithlessness.

I strive for success and am fractured by failure.
I reach for eternal joy
        and am clobbered with depression.
I wait for guidance,
        and Your heavens are gray with silence.
I ask for Your Spirit
        and am confronted with emptiness.
I seek opportunities
        and run into stone walls.

I overcome these pernicious demons
            in the morning
        only to face them again
            when day turns into night.
They refuse to die, these persistent devils.
They plague my days and haunt my nights
        and rob me of the peace and joy
            of God-motivated living.
And yet, O Lord, You have surrounded my life
        like a great fortress.

There is nothing that can touch me
   save by Your loving permission.
My faith will falter at times,
   but You will never fail me.
Teach me, O God,
      to live by Your Word and promises,
      to sing Your praises,
      to carry on within Your purposes
      despite these taunting, tempting enemies
         of my soul.

60

You made us, O God, a great nation.
The lands beyond our own
    tremble at our awesome might.
But the rich wine of material wealth dulled our senses.
The tyranny of things obscured our vision.
We grew arrogant, self-satisfied,
    and were often insensitive to the needs
        of Your creatures beyond our borders.

We waved our swords menacingly
    at potential enemies of our great country.
We established our outposts
    in the very heart of our enemies' camps.
We extended our powerful tentacles
        into other nations' undeveloped resources
        and drew their blood into our own.
And we did this in Your name,
    and we convinced ourselves
        that it was by Your will.

Now our defenses have been broken, O Lord.
Our fortress has been breached.
We have given birth to offspring
    that threaten us from within.
Splinter groups within our boundaries
    assert their identity and threaten to destroy
        our trust in unity under the flag.

Disillusioned youth rebel against
    a seemingly hopeless future and create
        fear through might of ill-gotten and ill-used arms.
Buildings explode, innocent lives are taken,
    young blood is spilled over turf conflicts.
And as if the violence in the streets weren't enough,
    our religious institutions are under bombardment
      from New Age philosophies that
      subtly soften and erode our faith
      in the one true God.
We are becoming paralyzed by fear
    and polarized by the extreme actions
      of radical and reactionary people.

Your Word is clear
    for those who would follow You, O God.
Your promises are assured
    for the nation that will worship You.
The enemies that threaten us
    and the problems that beset us
can be absolved only when we return to our God.
    He will guide us
    and make us a blessing to the world.

We seek Your help, O Lord,
    in restoring our great nation.

Listen to me, O God,
     listen to what I have to say.
From the bowels of this fractured world,
     I cry out my fears and longings.

I cannot find peace or security
     until I lose myself in something or someone
          that is greater than I.
Draw me more deeply into Your life and purposes;
     only then will I find shelter from the tempests
          of this fearful and uncertain existence.

You know that I am committed to You.
And because I am committed,
     I have inherited the same divine promises
          that are given to all who follow You.
Grant me the grace
     to fulfill my pledge of loyalty and service,
     and I shall never cease to sing Your praises.

62

As for me, my heart waits on God.
I know that my salvation comes from Him.
I may change my views about many things,
    but as for my need for God and His love,
        that is one conviction
        that shall never change.

There are many who would like
    to sabotage a person's deepest convictions.
With the skillful use of words and logic,
    they try to destroy
        the very foundations of faith.
As for me, my heart waits on God.
He is my Hope and my Help.
The temporal values that people focus on
    are so quickly lost
        amid the tempests of this life.
Their highest aspirations
    burst forth like bright flares
        only to fizzle out like wet fuses.

But my God offers a security that is eternal.
It cannot be logically defined,
    but it can be experienced.
Commit your life to Him,
    and you shall discover an anchor that will hold firm
        despite the chaos of this existence
        or the prattle of defiant unbelievers.

63

Like a thirsty child reaching for a drink,
    I grasp for You, O God.
And I have found You.
I have sensed Your holy presence
        in the worship service;
    in the hour of prayer,
        I have felt You to be near.
I realize now that Your love for me
    is far better than life itself.

My heart is full of joy and contentment.
My mouth is filled with praises for You.
Even the night hours are no longer lonely
    as I contemplate Your tender concern for me.

The enemies of my soul still seek to betray me,
    but they shall not snatch me out of Your hand.
And now that I have found You,
    I shall be secure and happy forever.

64

Listen to me, O God,
   I think I have good reason to complain.

I try very hard to follow Your paths
   and to serve Your purposes.
But I am deeply disturbed
   about the enemies and pitfalls
      that I unsuspectingly meet
         around every corner.
I find them in the tumultuous passions
   of my own being.
Much as I seek
      to rid myself of these overwhelming forces,
   they continue to clutch at my soul
      and to trip me up as I strive to please You.
I become so tired of this perpetual conflict
   with my sin-permeated nature.

And then I run into opposition
   in the reactions of trusted friends.
Their suspicions and unjust criticisms
   leave me withered and dried up
      in depression and discouragement.

Now it is the cunning words of the worldly-wise
      and the intellectual giants of this age
   that threaten the very foundations
      of what I so intensely believe.

Renew my faith, O Lord, and strengthen my belief
that those who foolishly oppose You
will fail in their attempts
to thwart Your purposes.
Hold before me Your promise: Those who trust in You
are truly and eternally secure,
even amid continuous conflict and antagonism.

65

You well-deserve the praises of Your children, O God,
and they should fulfill their pledges to You.

Everyone must eventually face up to You,
and it must be with all
our sins and shortcomings.
But those who come in sorrow and repentance
shall find You merciful and gracious.
You, O Lord, shall forgive their sins
and fill their hearts with Your love and joy.

O God, You reach out to save us.
You are the single, eternal Hope of all humankind.

You make Your power known to us
in the majestic grandeur of the mountains,
in the thunderous roar of ocean waves.
Your abundance is poured out upon us
in the grain-laden fields,
in the flocks and herds in the meadows,
in the gentle rain that caresses the green hills.
Your love for us is manifested
in Your great acts of deliverance on our behalf.

You well-deserve the praises of Your children, O God.

66

It is high time we start making
    happy noises about God,
    that we boldly proclaim His name
    and shout His praises.

We already know
    what He has done throughout history,
      the great deeds He has performed,
      the people who witnessed them
        and worshiped Him.
Let us recognize, as well,
    what He is constantly doing for us.

He walks with us into the crucible of conflict.
    He tests and tries us
      in the valley of pain and sorrow.
    He allows us to taste the agony of affliction.
    He gives our enemies permission
      to oppose and oppress us.
And then He uses these very things
    to purge and prepare us for His purposes.

Now I renew my pledge to my God.
I strive to carry out those promises I made to Him
    when I cried for His help in my troubles.
I yield my life to Him
    as a sacrifice and thankoffering.

You who are seeking God,
    these are the things He has done for me:
He has accepted me despite my sins and failures.
He listens when I cry to Him,
    and He responds with solace and support.

I proclaim God's praises
    because I know He will love me forever.

67

May we continually be
    the recipients of God's mercy and blessing
so that we may demonstrate
    His order and purpose throughout the earth
and His redemptive power
    to the creatures of this world.

And may it ultimately result
    in all of God's sons and daughters
        lifting their voices in
            praise to their Lord and God.

The nations of the earth would truly
        abide in peace and sing for joy
    if God were to be their God
    and if they would direct their actions
        according to His will.
Then the inhabitants of this world would surely
    lift their voices in praise to their Lord and God.

The earth continues to receive
    the abundance of God.
His blessings are all around us.
May every mountain and valley, plain and forest,
    every city and every sprawling suburb
        echo with the praises of men and women
        to their God.

68

We long for the day when God will take over our land,
  when wickedness will be suppressed
    and selfishness subdued,
  when people will begin to care for one another.

There will be clean air to breathe
  and pure water to drink.
There will be better schools for the young,
  hospitals for all who are ill,
  and jobs for those who seek them.
Everyone will feel needed and loved—;
  the child, the laborer,
  the executive, the senior citizen.
There will be dignity and freedom and equal rights,
  no matter our ethnic or economic background.
There will be homes to live in
  and parks to play in.
There will be libraries and theaters
  and halls of learning.
There will be a place for everyone to live
  and work and learn and rest and play.
And people will have time for one another.

O how we will praise God in such a land!
Our voices will join in a great chorus of celebration.
Daily we will offer thanksgiving to our God,
  who rules over our land.
And everyone will have time for one another.

But God does not rule over our land.
Our streets are pregnant with crime.

The poor and dispossessed gather at
    shelters and food banks.
Our schools are overcrowded and inadequate.
We choke on the air we breathe.
We stumble over our own litter and waste.
We neglect the old and ignore the young.
We rush pell-mell from appointment to appointment.
And no one cares for one another.

You seek, O God, to rule over our land.
You have given us pure air and green hills
    and great forests and clean rivers.
You have showered us with Your abundant gifts—
    all that we need to make our land splendid.
And You have given us Your love
    and the command to care for one another.

We have failed You, O God.
    We have sucked to our individual bosoms
        the gifts of Your love,
    but we have never really learned
        how to care for one another.

You have rebuked us for our selfishness, O Lord.
We are smothering in the waste
    of our self-centered living.
Deliver us, O God,
    restore to us a land worthy of Your habitation,
    and teach us, O loving God,
        how to care for one another.

O God, at this time I find myself
   backed up against the wall,
      at the bottom of the barrel,
      at the end of my rope.
There is no place to go but up.
Save me, O God, before it is too late.

I can't even cry out any longer;
   I can't even pray, so deep is my despair.

O Lord, You know the ugliness of my failure.
How sorely it must grieve You!
Forbid that others may be hurt by my foolishness
   or that my errors and faults might lead them astray.
I have been trying to represent You to them;
   instead I have brought dishonor and disrespect
      to my witness and Your name.
Now even those who once loved me
      keep their distance;
   those who listened in respect
      turn away in disgust.

Maybe my intense
      eagerness to carry out Your purposes
         has become my stumbling block,
   and now I am being ridiculed for my zeal.
They make fun of me;
   they whisper about me behind my back.

O God, don't let me go down the drain.
Respond, in Your great love,
    to my unhappy plight.
Raise me from the mire of despair,
    the darkness of depression.
Deliver me from these human weaknesses
        that plague me and lead me into defeat.
You know what they are, O Lord,
    and You know the limits of my endurance.
You know, as well, the pain of my failure
    and the abject loneliness I feel
        when I lose the battle.

You know, O God,
    and You reach forth in mercy
        to rescue and deliver.
You sometimes permit failure
    and defeat in my life
    so that my relationship with you
        can be revived and renewed.
Thus I again will sing the praises of God
    and make thankofferings to Him.

May all those who are
        beaten down by failure and despair
    see anew Your love
    and experience Your deliverance
    and be restored once more
        to joy and purposefulness.

70

O God, may You take pleasure in setting me free
and in securing me
from the enemies of my soul.
Keep them from bringing
shame upon Your servant
and dishonor to Your name.

May those who sincerely seek You
find genuine happiness and fulfillment,
and may they express their joy
in proclamations of praise to You.
As for me, I always
need Your sustaining grace.
O God, do not withhold it from me.

Good Lord, You have kept me
within the secure embrace of Your love
these many years.
My life is one long list of divine deliverances.
I have come running to You again and again
when the forces of evil
set themselves against me.

From the moment of my birth,
I was dedicated to Your will,
given life by You
only to yield it back to You.
And since that time, the days and hours of my life
have been filled with praise for You.

But the enemies that plagued me in my youth
still lay siege to my soul,
looking for chinks in my armor,
for loopholes in my defenses,
through which to enter and lay waste.

Now, as I near
the late afternoon and evening of my life,
I continue to seek Your love and mercy.
Even while I shout Your praises
and proclaim Your salvation,
I reach for the assurance
of Your love and concern.

You have guided me
      through my precarious youth,
      now I need Your grace for my senior years.
Fill my heart with purpose
      and my mouth with praises
      so that I may continue to proclaim
         Your name and Your salvation
            to all who will listen.

You are, O God, the Creator and Performer
      of great and glorious things.
There is no one like You.
You have kept me safe throughout life's conflicts,
      led me through its crucible of experiences,
      drawn me back from its pitfalls and precipices,
      healed all my wounds,
         and comforted me in my afflictions.
Thus I know that You
      will continue to love and care for me.

I will dedicate my remaining days
      to praising You,
         espousing Your faithfulness,
         and proclaiming Your love and concern
            for all who will turn to You.
May every fiber of my being and
      every activity of my life
         resound with praises to my God.

72

O God of love,
   grant to Your children the grace
      to represent You effectively
      in our discordant world.
Give us the courage
      to put our lives on the line
   to communicate life and truth
      to all Your creatures,
         wherever they may be found.

Where there is injustice,
      may we diagnose its cause
      and discover its cure.
Where there is bigotry,
      teach us how to love
      and how to encourage others to love.
Where there is poverty,
      help us share the wealth
         that has come from Your hand.
Where there is war and violence,
      make us peacemakers that lead
      men and women to Your eternal peace.

Help us, O God, to become what You
      have appointed and empowered us to become.
Where there is darkness,
      may we become the rays of Your sun
         that banish the gloom from lonely lives.
Where there is drought,
      let us be like gentle showers
         that turn barren deserts into green meadows.

Where there is ugliness and distortion,
　　enable us to portray the beauty and order
　　of Your will and purposes.

Great God, You are in our world.
Your majesty is reflected
　　in Your creation around us.
But there are multitudes who do not
　　feel Your concern
　　　or acknowledge Your love.
Is it because Your servants have failed
　　to carry out Your command and commission?
　　or that we have yet to sense
　　　the significance of our salvation
　　　and the purpose of our mission?

Forbid, O God,
　　that we be deaf to the cries of the poor
　　　or indifferent to those who have needs.
May we identify with those who are oppressed
　　and help bear the burdens
　　　of those who suffer.
May we hear Your voice of concern
　　and feel Your loving touch
　　　and as Your servants in this world,
　　　manifest You to people around us.
The glory is Yours, O God,
　　and we shall praise Your name
　　　and celebrate Your cause together.

73

It is generally expected
    that God will stand by the righteous
    and remain close to those whose thoughts and deeds
        are purely altruistic.
I am afraid I just don't belong
    to that class of people.
I guess I am just a perpetual backslider.
Rather than thinking unselfishly,
    I find myself envious and covetous
        of those who have so much more than I do.

They never seem to have problems.
They are always so strong and healthy.
I doubt that they know the meaning of conflict.
They are proud, carefree,
    and so disgustingly smug about everything.
They act as if God didn't even exist,
    and they are almost blasphemous
        in their attitudes and actions.

And yet people honor and applaud them;
    they find nothing to censor about them.
What aggravates me is the obvious unconcern
    about God or others.
Yet they always appear to be
    so comfortable and well-off.

And all the while I struggle so desperately
    with my sin-permeated nature.

I try so hard to please God,
   yet my days are full of conflict,
      and my heart seethes in unrest.

I know I speak foolishly and unfairly,
   but I get so fed up with it all.
That is, until I begin arguing with God about it.
Then I realize that those who are materially rich are
      not as well-off as they appear.
Their bright bubble will burst some day;
   their dream will turn into a nightmare.

It's just that I get so depressed at times,
   and I act like a stupid fool.
It amazes me that even while engrossed
      in irrational and unspiritual contemplations,
   I am never far from You, O Lord.
You hold me close to Yourself.
You guide me and watch over me.
You assure me that it is all worth it.
And because of this glorious truth,
   I have no need for anything else.
The essential desires of my being are met in You, O God.
I shall be victimized often by human failure,
   but my great God never ceases
      to love me and bless me.

How good it is to know that God is always near!

74

It disturbs and discourages me, O God,
  to witness the apparent successes
    of those who oppose You.
While Your children wrestle
    with doubts and conflicts,
      the agnostics and false religious leaders of our world
      tear down the pillars of our faith
      and gloat over our frustration.

They make fun of our rituals and symbols.
They dissect our dogmas
    and ridicule our institutions.
They create godless philosophies
    that seduce the young and confuse the old.

They deliberately obstruct our efforts
    to represent You in our world.
As a result of their diabolical activities,
    many have turned away from the true God
      to worship lesser gods
      and to chase after lesser goals.

We know, O God, how You have handled
    Your enemies in the past.
We know that You cannot be dethroned,
    that You are God over all creation.
Then how can You allow these God-defiers
    to get by with what they are doing?

Consider our restlessness, O God.
Do not let them step on us and grind us under their feet.
Help us, O God,
        ineffective and foolish as we may be,
    to stand up to the demigods
        that plague our land.

75 AND 76

We praise You, O God.
Even in the midst of this world's wickedness,
    we celebrate Your majesty and power.

For You are here, O God.
You are here to save;
    You are here also to judge.
Even while the godless trumpet their rebellion,
    You hold the world in the palm of Your hand.
Should You close Your hand in anger, O God,
        their doom is sealed,
        their boasts ended forever.

Your fainthearted servants
    need not be dismayed, O God.
Even the rebelliousness of these obstinate creatures
    can serve to further Your purposes.
We need not fear the distortions
    of those who defy and oppose You.
We need only renew our relationship with You,
    rededicate our lives to Your objectives,
    and continue to celebrate Your presence
        and Your power in our world.

I cry to God in my desperation.
Out of the dark corner of my stifling loneliness,
   I grope in vain for some solace or comfort.

I try to think about God,
      to contemplate His many promises,
         but my heart is empty,
         my soul as dry as dust.
I spend sleepless nights searching,
      waiting for God to speak to my need,
         to give me strength in my conflict.
I remember how He has responded
         to my prayers in times past,
      but I get nothing from Him now—
         nothing except the echoes of my own agonized
         screams to the empty heavens.

I am reminded of His deeds
      and wonders of years past,
      how He demonstrated His love
         and concern for His people.
His majesty and power are reflected
      in the great forces of nature.
Then why doesn't He hear my pitiful pleadings?
Why doesn't He fulfill His promises to me?
Good Lord, where are You?

78

It would be good for us to consider God's dealings
    with people and nations throughout history.
We ought to know these things;
    we have heard them again and again.
But we forget so quickly,
    and we fall so foolishly into the same pitfalls
        of infidelity and purposelessness.

God reached down and gathered a people for Himself.
He drew them into His fortress of love.
He revealed Himself to them
        through His commandments,
            which taught them how to live together in peace.
He enabled them to sense His presence
        in miraculous ways.
He poured out on them
        all that was needed to sustain them.
Even in the barren desert,
        food was rained on them from heaven,
        and water burst forth
            from the rocks around them.
He sent prophets to teach them
        and warriors to guide them
            through enemy country.
Like a shepherd who watches over his flock,
        our Lord watched over His children.

But like silly, confused sheep,
        the children of God went astray.

They became self-sufficient and wandered off
    to pursue their own selfish interests.
Many of them rebelled against their God.
They refused His love and would not
    walk in His paths.

They became lost in the desert.
They suffered sorely for their sins.
They knew hunger and thirst and fear.
Only then did they remember
    the Creator of their youth
    and the loving care their heavenly Father provided
        when they walked in His paths.

Some of them turned back to God.
They discovered once more their loving God,
    a God willing to forgive them and accept them,
        to gather them once more
        into His fortress of love—
    to care for them and watch over them
        like a shepherd over his flock.

Like silly, selfish sheep,
    we often wander off on our own,
        imagining that we can find
        our own way to joy and security.
We discover pain and emptiness and meaninglessness
        outside the orbit of God.

We are out of joint,
    and the deepest longings of our hearts
      go unfulfilled.

I return, O God, to You
    and Your purposes for my life.
I find You waiting for me,
    ready to forgive my foolishness
    and my rebelliousness and eager
      to reinstate me in Your family
      and reconcile me to Your will once more.

I thank You, O God,
    for drawing me back to Your loving heart.

79

Why is it, O Lord,
　　that the ungodly appear to be so successful?
They have no use for the church.
They play fast and loose with the lives of others.
They live solely for themselves
　　and have no concern for individuals
　　　　except to use them
　　　　　　to further their personal ambitions.
They not only obstruct Your purposes, God,
　　they pollute Your world and taunt Your servants.

Why do You let them do it, O Lord?
Why don't You seek satisfaction from Your enemies?
Why don't You show them,
　　through Your faithful servants,
　　that success comes to those
　　　　who love and follow You?
　　that we are on the right course?

Help me, O God, to love Your enemies
　　even as You love them,
　　to bear patiently and graciously their scorn,
　　and to serve You faithfully
　　　　whatever the consequences.
Help me measure my worth and success
　　by Your standards
　　and rejoice in Your love and acceptance.

80

O God, You are the Creator
and the Sustainer of Your church.
You have protected and prospered
Your faithful followers
throughout the stormy and tumultuous past.

Today we are in trouble.
Listen to our cries of consternation, O God.
We are confused and confounded.
We don't know where to turn,
in what direction to go.

We have prayed, O God.
We have sung Your praises.
We have proclaimed Your love to the world.
But today our power is slipping away,
our prestige is wearing thin.
People seem to have little respect for us anymore.
Those who have been brought up
within our structures
and have embraced our doctrines
are leaving the fold.
They say we no longer meet their needs
or the needs of the world.

You were with us in the beginning, Lord.
You planted us in the midst
of this world's turmoil.
You nurtured us and watched over us.

Despite the enemies
        who sought to destroy us,
    we grew until we encircled the earth.
Great halls of worship were built in Your honor, Lord.
Magnificent institutions were established
        to carry out Your purposes.
Men and women dedicated their lives
        to proclaim Your teachings.
Multitudes gathered to declare Your praises.

Today we are in trouble, Lord.
The walls are crumbling.
Our sanctuaries no longer attract the masses.
People dedicate their lives to other purposes.
We no longer make much of an impression
        on this world of ours.

Renew Your church, O God.
We know You will never turn away
        those who come to You
        and will forever sustain
        those who trust in You.
Fan the dying embers, Lord.
Stir us up and restore us to a position
        of power and effectiveness.
Give us new life and new vision
        so we may advance Your kingdom
        in our disjointed world.
Renew Your church, O God,
        and revive Your servants
        so the whole earth may know of Your love.

81 AND 82

Our great God has heard our cry,
    and He is speaking to His church today.
He reminds us that He is the God of our world,
    the God who piloted His people through history,
      who regards His church with love and concern.
He would remind us
    that He freed us from sin's burden and guilt,
    that He responded to our pleas for deliverance
    and was present with us
    in the trials and conflicts of our lives.
He would remind us of the many times
    we neglected to listen to Him
    and how He had to allow us to hurt ourselves
    because we stubbornly chose our own course.
He reiterates His promise to meet our needs
    and to enrich our lives
    as we rely on Him for grace and strength.
He diagnoses our sickness even today
    and points us to His purpose for our existence.

We have become complacent
    in our structures and institutions.
We have been subtly diverted
    from His will and purposes in our world.
We have selfishly interpreted His Word
    to fit our schemes and carry out our intents.
We have clutched at God to pacify and sustain us
    even while we remain insensitive to the
      suffering world around us.

Now God is speaking again,
    in judgment as well as with promise.
He is reaching out to restore us to Himself
    and to renew our vision for His world.
"How long will you ignore
    My oppressed and dispossessed children,
    their cries for liberty and justice?"
      our God is saying to the church.
"Why do people go hungry around you
    while you abound in gifts from My hand?
You are My children and My servants,
    My representatives in a fractured world.
I can reach those sick, needy, loveless,
    and lonely creatures only through you.
This is the reason I have given you so much,
    that you may share it with others."

Help us, O God,
    to return to Your purposes for Your church,
    to recognize all Your creatures as Your subjects,
      to remember that the world belongs to You.
May Your great love and grace flood our lives
    and overflow to touch with healing
    the lives of every one of Your children.

You are in our world, O God.
May we serve You here by ministering
    to the needs of those around us.

83

I am so depressed tonight, O God.
I feel like I am the sole target
    of an enemy barrage—
        like all the demons of hell are bent
            on damning my soul for eternity.

I remember Your precious promises,
    but I do not witness their fulfillment.
I talk to people about Your love,
    and they drown my zeal with scorn.
I step forth to carry out Your will,
    but I feel no sense of accomplishment.
I mouth words, wave my arms,
    and beat the air in fruitless endeavor.
Then I fall like a wounded warrior,
    bone-weary, defeated, and lonely.
And I wonder if You are truly my God
    and if I am really Your child.

Consume, O God, these demons that depress,
    these enemies that plague my soul.
May the whirlwind of Your Spirit
    sweep them out of my life forever.
May I awaken with a heart full of joy
    and with the strength and courage
        to walk straight and secure
            in the dangerous
            and difficult paths before me.

84

O God, the center of Your will
is truly the place of fulfillment.
I long continuously
for the peace and security of walking with You.
Therein lies the sole purpose and meaning for my life.

Even the birds of the air
and the animals that inhabit land and sea
abide within Your orbit and plan for them.
Thus it is that men and women
who follow Your course for them
are forever blessed.

How enriched are those
who draw their power from You,
whose hearts are focused on You!
Even as they wend their way
through this fractured world,
they become springs of healing,
reservoirs of strength,
to the sick, weak, and empty lives
they touch around them.

O Lord, look with loving mercy upon those
who have placed their lives in Your hands.
Just one day in the center of Your will
is incomparably better than a thousand
spent in the pursuit
of self-centered aims and objectives.

It is more fulfilling to be an underpaid clerk
    in the service of my God
    than to be the owner and director
        of some huge, wealthy enterprise.

O God, nothing that is truly good and worthwhile
    is withheld from those who walk
        within Your will.
The person who trusts You is very rich indeed.

85

O God, You indeed have been good to us.
You have prospered our land.
You have opened Your heart to us in love.
You have forgiven our sins
    and adopted us as Your sons and daughters.

But our country is in turmoil.
We no longer have confidence in our leaders.
Some segments of society feel
    disenfranchised and display their
    displeasure in open revolt.
Our young people spill blood
    in turf wars and over drugs.
People are turning away from You
    only to be ensnared
      by false doctrines
      and godless philosophies.

We know that You have not turned away from us.
You touch with joy and peace
    the hearts that belong to You.
You stand ready to show Your salvation.
    to all who will trust in You.
As we speak to You in faith,
    You respond with loving concern.
You will give us what is good
    and will prosper us
      with gifts from Your hand.

You are holy and just.
You love Your children and will guide them
    in Your course for their lives.

Renew our faith, O God.
Forgive our many failures and infidelities.
May our land continue to be a place
    where we are free to love and serve You.

86

O Lord, my prayer to You always comes
   out of a life full of need.
I am Your servant;
   I am trying to represent You.
I need Your support for every step I take.
How gracious You are to hear my plea
   and respond to my cry
   and pour out Your forgiving love upon me!

People are so foolish
   about the things they love and worship.
You alone are God,
   and You alone possess the healing grace
      that can support and sustain fickle hearts.
Continue to lead me in Your course for my life.
Enable me to walk, body and soul,
   in loving obedience to You.
Then I shall glorify You forever,
   and my life shall be
      a continual thankoffering to You.

I find the daily journey
   not only difficult but painful.
There are forces within me and around me
   that overpower me.
But You are a loving and patient God.

Continue to have mercy upon me,
    to stir me from the doldrums of sin,
    to deliver me from selfish involvements,
    to forgive my sins and failures,
    to shore up the weak places in my life.
Help me
    feel Your loving acceptance
    and reflect to others
        the joy of being Your child and servant.

87

This world is God's world.
And our great God loves the world that He made
and the people He created to inhabit it.
Living in teeming cities or remote villages,
they are all God's people,
and His love embraces each and every one.

Not all the men and women of this world
are citizens of the kingdom of God.
The people who shun His redeeming love
cannot inhabit the city of eternal light.
They become the children of darkness.
They shall wander forever
through the limitless spaces of nothingness.

The sons and daughters of God enjoy
a close relationship with their
Father and Creator.
They walk in obedience to His will and Word.
They shall dwell together in joy
and shall sing and dance
in continuous celebration
in that beautiful city
beyond the boundaries and borders
of this present world.

O God, I need You every day that I exist
and every night that I pass through.
Never turn Your face from me, O Lord,
for my life is a continuous plea for help.

My life is one long series of conflicts and defeats,
and they only increase as I near its end.
My ultimate destiny is a hole in the ground,
but even now I am as good as dead.
Without strength, forsaken,
shunned by those around me,
I feel as if I were separated forever from You.
I am assailed by afflictions,
attacked by obsessions,
and all but forgotten by God and human beings.

And yet I continue to cry out to You.
Even while the assaults of this life
and the fear of death
surround me and close in on me,
I look to You for some ray of hope.

Good Lord, where are You?
Is there nothing within me worth saving?

89

I feel like singing this morning, O Lord.
I feel like telling everyone around me
    how great You are.
If only they could know the depths of Your love
    and Your eternal concern for those
        who follow You!
But my songs are so often off-key.
My speech is so inadequate.
I simply cannot express what I feel,
    what I know to be true about Your love
        for Your creatures upon this world.

But even the songs of the birds
    proclaim Your praises.
The heavens and the earth beneath them,
        the trees that reach toward You,
        the flowers that glow in colorful beauty,
        the green hills and soaring mountains,
        the valleys and the plains,
        the lakes and the rivers,
        the great oceans that pound the shores—
    they proclaim Your greatness, O God,
    and Your love for Your human creatures
        throughout this world.

How glorious it is to be alive, O Lord!
May every breath of my body,
    every beat of my heart,
        be dedicated to Your praise and glory.

O God, You have always been God.
Long before the earth was formed,
    long after it ceases to exist,
    You have been and You shall always be.

With You there is no beginning or end;
    time is not measured by decades or centuries.
Our lives, so precious and important to us,
    are only fleeting shadows to You.
And they are full of trouble and conflict
    and marked by sin and failure.

O God, break into our short span of existence
    with Your eternal love and grace.
Intersperse our days of despair
    with hours of joy.
Enable us
    to see Your will and purpose
        for our presence here
    and to discover some meaning
        for our brief, trouble-fraught
            appearance in this world.
Imprint on us Your brand of ownership,
    and place us
        within Your plan and objective for our lives.

91

Those who focus their faith on God,
     who find their security in Him,
     do not have to live in fear.
They are not left untouched
     by the tempests of this life,
     and they may be wounded
     by the onslaughts of evil,
     but their great God does not leave them
     to suffer these things alone.
The Lord cares for His own and delivers them
     even in the midst of the conflicts
     that plague them.

If God is truly your God,
     you do not have to be afraid
     of the enemy that threatens
     or the affliction that lays you low.
Men and women all around you may fall,
     never to rise again,
     but the Lord is by your side
     to raise you to your feet
     and to lead You to ultimate victory.

Even the ministering spirits of His invisible world
     watch over you.
They will not let anything hurt you
     except by God's loving permission
     and through His eternal concern.

Our loving God has promised:
"Because My children love Me,
   I will never let them go.
I shall feel the pain of their wounds
     and bear their hurt
    and shall transform that which is ugly
      into that which enriches and blesses.
And when they cry out in agony,
   I shall hear and answer them.
I will be close to them and will deliver them,
    and I will grant them eternal life."

92

It's a glorious feeling to be able
    to unload my heart,
    to spill out my gratitude
        in thanks to You, O God.
Morning, noon, and night,
    I want the whole world to know of Your love.
I want to shout it, to sing it,
    in every possible way
        to proclaim Your praises,
        to express my joy.

How great You are, O Lord!
Your thoughts are unfathomable,
    Your ways beyond comprehension.
And all the while, the problem of evil
    still confounds us.
We simply cannot understand
    why the ungodly appear to be so successful,
    why good fortune seems to follow those
        who defy You.
But we know their success is short-lived.
Those who refuse to turn to You will never find
    that ultimate and total fulfillment
        that is promised to the children of God.

The children of God,
        those whose lives are open to You,
        portray the wonder and beauty of Your Spirit.

They are like springs of water in a parched world.
They flourish even amid the distortions
　　and the ugliness around them.
Their lives are rich and productive
　　in a barren and desolate society.

Help us, those of us who love You, O God,
　　to prove to our disjointed world
　　　that You are in our midst.

93

It may not always be apparent,
    but God does reign over our world.
He rules in majesty and might,
    and no philosophy or power
        can cast Him from His throne.

He allows us to cross up His purposes—
    even to destroy His visible creation.
But His place and His reign are eternally secure.
And so are they who put their trust in Him,
    who live by His precepts,
        and who follow His course for their lives.

It is difficult, O God, to understand
how You can ignore Your enemies
as they persist in thwarting Your purposes
and abusing Your children in this world.
They provoke me to anger, O Lord.
How can You withhold Your vengeance?

Even those of us who name Your name
and sing Your praises
are often indifferent to or careless about
the needs of those around us.
We stand indicted, Lord.
Our calloused self-centeredness has perpetuated
the wars and poverty and bigotry
that abound in our society.
We don't hate people, Lord,
we just don't really care about them.

Is it possible, O Lord, that we are Your enemies?
That we are thwarting Your purposes
and abusing Your children in this world?
We are busy with good works, Lord.
We build churches and send out missionaries
and establish schools and hospitals
and homes for the elderly.
But we don't like the poor, Lord,
or the people who can't speak our language,
or those who don't appreciate our patronizing gifts.

They frighten us when they reach out
        for the fruits of our labor,
            our affluence, our respectability,
            our right to be wealthy
            and comfortable and secure.
Sometimes, Lord, we just don't like people.
Why don't they leave us alone
        so we can love and serve You in peace?

Thank You, God, for not pouring out Your wrath
        on those who are disobedient to You.
We have been Your enemies at times.
Even while we worship
        in our comfortable sanctuaries,
        we may stand in Your way.
And thank You, God,
        because You love even Your enemies,
            and through Your chastisement
            may transform them into
            Your sons and daughters.

Strike the scales from our eyes, O Lord,
        that we may see Your handwriting on the wall
            and accept Your chastening love
            and return to You in repentance and faith.
Strike the shackles from our hearts and hands
        that we may reach out to demonstrate
            and to relate Your love
            to Your children around us.

95

Let us begin this day with singing.
Whether we feel like it or not,
    let us make glad sounds
        and force our tongues to articulate words
        of thanksgiving and praise.

The facts are: God is with us;
    this world and we who live in it are His;
    He loves us;
    He has adopted us as His children;
    we belong to Him.
This makes us valid, worthwhile.
We are truly significant in the eyes of our God
    despite our human feelings
        or the comments of our critics.

This may not be the way we feel this morning,
    but this is the way it is.
We don't need the plaudits of our peers—
    we have God's stamp of approval.

So let us begin this day with singing
    whether we feel like it or not.
Then we may end this day with praises
    because we know—and may even feel—
        that we shall forever be
            the objects of God's concern
            and the children of His love.

96

God is here; God is now!
It is time for celebration!
Our praises need not be confined to old songs.
Nor do we need great organs or massive choirs
    to honor His name.
Let us create new songs of praise to our God.
Let us discover new ways of proclaiming
    His greatness and glory!

The elements around us reflect His majesty.
The roaring sea and all that inhabits it,
        the wind that bends the trees,
        the creatures that fill the air and land,
        the mountains that probe our skies,
        the rivers and lakes that slake our thirst,
        the great planets and stars
            that light up our night—
all these reveal God's beauty and splendor.
And out of this comes that fashioned
    by human mind and body:
        art, architecture, music, literature,
        and the inventions of science.

Wherever one turns,
        God's power is manifested,
        God's presence is made apparent.
Let us celebrate His presence
    in our world today.

97

I can't even see the sun this morning.
The coastland fog has blotted out heaven's light,
    making the early hours cold and damp.
But God is here—in me and around me—
    and I will rejoice in Him.

I hear no angel choirs.
No church bells summon me to worship.
Only the thunder of four-wheel vehicles
        and the acrid odor of exhaust greet me
    as men and women rush to their unnumbered shrines
        and pursue their avaricious goals.
But God is here, and I will rejoice in Him.

I cannot see the mountains or smell the flowers
    or even hear the songs of birds.
I cannot love the people who bustle around me.
I see unhappiness and injustice and depravity.
I hear the ear-grating sounds of pain and complaint.
I feel the stifling pressures that suck me
    into the stream that rushes by my door.
But God is here—in me and around me—
    and I will rejoice in Him.

Our great God does care for His creatures.
He secures forever those who are His.
He is here—in us and around us.
Let us all rejoice in Him!

98

Men and women have proclaimed God's praises
   throughout the ages.
Now it is our turn to worship the Lord
   and to announce God's presence
      and His loving concern
      to the inhabitants of this world.
His power is as great today as it ever was.
He continues to reign over His universe
   and the creatures that move in this world.
He alone is the true God.
He offers to all men and women His salvation.
He is close to His children and servants
   and fills their hearts with joy.

Now, as His children and servants,
   let us express this joy.
With voice and musical instruments,
      with lovely melodies and joyful sounds,
   let us proclaim the glory of God.
Let us fill our homes and sanctuaries,
   our halls of learning,
   our factories and marketplaces,
   even the streets of our city,
      with sounds of celebration.
God is here; God is now!

The Lord does reign over this world!
Even when the earth quakes
    and fires rage through the forests
    and floods inundate the lowlands
    and human beings and their creations are laid low,
  God is Lord and Master over all the earth.

The Lord does reign over this world!
Even when people turn against one another
    and nations engage in war
    and violence and injustice are heaped
    on His creatures,
  God is Lord and Master over all the earth.

God's creatures bear the consequences
    of their self-centeredness,
  and this world is distorted by their depravity.
But the Lord forgives those who turn to Him
  and makes them His children and His servants
  and through them seeks to heal
    this world's gaping wounds
  and the hurts that people inflict upon one another.

The Lord establishes relationships with those who
  call upon Him.
The priests and prophets of history
  heard His voice
  and followed His course for their lives.

His servants and disciples of this hour
    sense His presence
    and communicate His love and grace
    to those who reach out for Him.

The Lord does reign over this world!
He is Lord and Master over all the earth.

100

Break forth
  into exclamations of joy and gladness,
  you who serve the Lord!

God is not dead! He is ever our God!
He made us, we belong to Him;
  we are His children and servants.
And His love for us never runs out;
  His care and concern for us will go on forever.

Let the world see our manifestations of joy!
Let us lift up our voices in songs of praise
    and surrender our lives
      as continual offerings of thanksgiving!
Let us bless His name forever!

101

O God, I love those hymns
    that speak of loyalty and justice,
    those prayers for the deprived and oppressed—
    even while I deprive and oppress my fellow persons
    through my apathy and egocentricity.

I embrace the old creeds that tell of Your love
        and the commandments that instruct me
        to reflect that love to others—
    even while I turn inward
    and allow bigotry and prejudice
        to color my relationships
        with those outside my private little club.
I treasure those promises I made in the sanctuary,
        those vows and solemn pledges before the altar—
    even while I flirt with this world's gods
        and bow before manmade shrines.
I decry the distortions of our world,
        the poverty and pain and indignities
        suffered by multitudes
        of this world's citizens—
    even while I stand aloof
        and wait for people's sorry needs
        to be met by others
    and brazenly oppose those remedies
        that may result in personal deprivation.

I avoid the sinner
and belittle the proud
and stand clear of cheaters and liars
and choose as my companions
the qualified and respected
members of my society.
And all the while I claim to be Your child
and to walk in Your ways.

Have mercy upon me, O God,
for I am a selfish and self-centered creature!

102

Good Lord, where are You?
If You really do exist,
    why don't You come out of hiding and
        do something about this creature in distress?

I am physically weary.
I am mentally depressed.
I am spiritually defeated.
I can't eat, can't sleep.
I am like garbage,
    discarded refuse in the back alley;
    like yesterday's newspaper,
        shuffled around by the wind.
I feel like some sort of zombie,
    some nonentity,
    some nothing that people,
        if they acknowledged me,
    would only curse.
I eat crow and drink gall.
Now even You have tossed me aside
    like some moth-eaten garment
        that no one could possibly want.

But the prophets have proclaimed Your name,
    and the Scriptures declare Your mercy,
    and the saints pass on Your promises.
You do reign over our world, they say.
    You do show concern
        for the poor clods of this earth.

Good Lord, prove it!
Look down from wherever You are
    on Your creatures wallowing in wretchedness.
Deliver us, O God, set us free!

I must take comfort in Your everlastingness—
    that You, who outlive seasons and centuries,
        who have blessed the saints of the past,
        can also care for Your servants
        in this fearful hour.
For Your years have no end
    nor do the lives of those who trust in You.

103

My heart bursts with praises to God;
    every fiber of my being reaches out in rejoicing!
How can I ever forget His many blessings?
    He forgives all my sins;
    He touches my afflictions with healing;
    He snatches me back
      from the gaping jaws of hell;
    He covers me with concern and love;
    He fulfills my deepest desires and gives me
      meaning for life and purpose for living.

God is a God of judgment and justice,
    but He sides with those who need His help.
He is angry with those
      who persistently rebel against Him,
    but He pours out His love
      on those who turn to Him.
He does not give us our just desserts
    or pay us what we well deserve.
He is grieved when we so miserably fail,
    but He quickly draws us to His forgiving heart
      and accepts us just as if it never happened.
He looks with tenderness
    at His faltering children;
    He knows and understands our fallible natures.

God's human creatures are pitiful
        pictures of weakness.
Now and then one will,
        like a streaking meteor,
    blaze out across the skies of time
        only to become a smoking cinder
        at the end of the short journey.
But those who are joined
        to God's loving will and purposes
    become the objects
        of His eternal mercy and righteousness.

Rejoice with me
        you who are His invisible servants
        and you who hear and obey His voice.
Shout His praises
    you who are His children
    and you who serve
        as His ministers and priests.
There is no time for despair and discouragement.
Whoever and wherever you are,
        lift your hearts in praises to God.

104

O Lord, how great and all-powerful You are!
And how beautiful is the world You created
    for our habitation!
Even before Adam was brought forth from the dust,
    or Eve was brought forth from Adam's rib,
    You prepared for them a place
        in which to live and grow.
And everything they saw around them
    reflected the beauty and power
        of the living God.

There was clean air.
Pure water from snowcapped mountains
    flowed through green valleys
    and gathered together in great lakes.
The skies shone with a million lights.
The land brought forth flowers and fruits
    to delight the eye and palate of God's creatures.
And every part of the land
    and the waters that covered the land
    and the skies that looked down on the land
        were filled with uncountable forms of life;
        the world was vibrant and alive.

Your power and Your beauty were spread
        throughout the universe,
    but it was only upon the heart of
        human creatures that You imprinted Your image.

And these creatures,
 in their short stay on this world,
 were appointed to be Your coworkers
 in the ever-continuing process of creation.
Your creative activity has never ceased.
It continues in and through their lives.

Limited and lowly as Your human creatures are,
 their minds and their hands are assigned
 to control Your life-giving process
 and to direct the maintenance and
 replenishment of the earth
 that life might be given and sustained
 throughout the world.

O Lord, how great and all-powerful You are!
And how beautiful is the world You created
 for our habitation!

105

How great is my God,
    and how I love to sing His praises!
Whereas I am often frightened
        when I think about the future
    and confused and disturbed
        by the rapidly changing world around me,
    my heart is secured and made glad
        when I remember how God has cared for me
            throughout the past.

When I came from my mother's womb,
    God's hand was on me.
Through parents and people who cared,
    He loved and sheltered me
        and set me on His course for my life.
Through illness and accident,
    my God has sustained me.
Around pitfalls and precipices
    He has safely led me.
When I became rebellious
        and struck out on my own,
    He waited patiently for me to return.
When I fell on my face in weakness and failure,
    He gently set me on my feet again.
He did not always prevent me from hurting myself,
    but He comforted me and healed my wounds.
Even out of the broken pieces of my defeats,
    He created a vessel of beauty and usefulness.

Through trials and errors, failures and successes,
   my God has cared for me.
From infancy to adulthood,
   He has never let me go.
His love has led me—or carried me—
   through the valleys of sorrow
      and the highlands of joy,
   through times of want
      and years of abundance.
He has bridged impassable rivers
   and moved impossible mountains.
Sometimes through me,
      sometimes despite me,
   He seeks to accomplish His purposes in my life.

He has kept me through the stormy past;
   He will secure and guide me
      through the perilous future.
I never need to be afraid,
   no matter how uncertain
      the months or years ahead of me.
How great is my God,
   and how I love to sing His praises!

106

I praise God today!
How exciting it is to be His child and servant!
What amazes me
    is the manner in which He makes
        hay out of the straw and stubble
    of my feeble efforts and foolish errors.

This is the way God deals with all His children.
We have so often fallen away from His love
    and accepted His gifts
        without respect or concern for the Giver.
We spout gratitude
    when some great deliverance
        comes our way:
    a successful surgery, a return to health,
    a financial bonus, a debt erased,
    a reconciliation with a loved one.
But when the crisis passes and calm is restored,
    we return to our old tricks,
        walk in our old ways,
        pursue our self-centered goals,
    with little concern for God's
        way and will for our lives.

We rejoice when God smiles on us,
    and sound off
        about how good and gracious He is.

But when we meet up with hard times
        or become enslaved
    to the boredom of the daily routine,
    we lapse into grumbling and griping
        and act as if God were a million miles away.

How loving and patient is my God!
Even when I fail Him,
    He never fails to love and care for me.
I so often limit Him
    with my inability to trust Him,
    my unwillingness to obey Him,
    my apathy, my self-concern,
    or my pursuit of the foolish
        goals and ambitions of this life.
And yet my God never ceases to pursue me,
    to draw me back into His circle of love,
    and to carry out His purposes
        even through the failures and defeats
        of my life.

How I praise God today!
How I pray that He may find pleasure
    in my love for Him!

107

Those who have experienced
the redemption of God
and know what it means
to be reconciled to Him
ought to dedicate their lives to serving Him
and their voices to proclaiming
to the world His loving grace.

Some of you have known
the meaning of emptiness and loneliness.
You have drunk from many wells
and sipped honey from many flowers
and stumbled into many blind alleys
in your search for fulfillment.
But your hearts remained empty and unsatisfied.
Then you faced up to God
and His claim on you,
and you discovered purpose and objective
for your lives.
Don't keep it to yourselves!
Tell it to the world!
Proclaim in word and deed
the wonderful works of a loving God.
Let others know that He is able
to fill their emptiness and satiate
their hunger.

Some of you have endured the long nights
of suffocating darkness.
You know well the dregs of depression,
the power of obsession,
the clutch of despair and frustration.

You fell on your faces in defeat,
    and no one seemed to care.
Then in desperation you cried out
        to God in your misery;
    and He flooded your lives with light and hope.
Thank God! It is by His eternal love
    that you are delivered.
Tell others about His power to deliver them
    from that which binds them or blinds them.

Some of you have followed
    sin's cruel consequences
        into the crucible of sickness and pain.
You were led to the very brink of destruction.
Then you turned to God in your great distress,
    and He touched you with His healing
        and delivered you from your afflictions.
Rejoice in God! Let your praises ascend to Him!
Proclaim His healing grace
    to others who may be ready to listen.

Some of you have set out in joyous abandon
    to find your happiness in the streets
        and marketplaces of the world.
But you became lost and disillusioned and afraid.
The exciting landscape became a devouring monster
    that threatened to dehumanize and destroy you.
You cried out for help,
    and you found that God was there
    among the milling masses.

He restored courage to your hearts
   and meaning to your lives.
You discovered purpose
   and validity and significance
      in the loving acceptance of your God.
Let the multitudes hear
   about your discovery!
Let them know that God is near
   that they may rejoice
      in His everlasting and ever-present love.
It is the lack of God in people's lives
   that dries them up and turns them into dust.
It is God's presence and acceptance
   that turns on the lights
   and floods the dark corridors that led nowhere
   and transforms them into warm rooms
   where one may live
      in joy and fulfillment.
It is the acknowledgment of a loving God
   that makes the forbidding world a place
      to live in
   and its God-fearing inhabitants
      glowing reflections of His eternal concern.

Great God, be it crowded street or solitary mountaintop,
   make it my pulpit
      from which to proclaim Your praises
   and my workbench from which to transmit
      Your love to the lives of lonely men and women.

108

My heart is glad today, O God,
    and I am determined to serve You!
I celebrate Your presence.
I glory in Your love for me.
I sing Your praises
    and yearn to proclaim Your loving concern to all.

The people I travel with have little feeling for You.
They act as if You do not exist.
They are empty.
Their lives have little meaning or purpose.
They bounce about in a vacuum,
    the deepest longings of their hearts unfulfilled.

I know to whom I belong,
    and I know where I am going.
I know that You are my Lord
    and that You will accompany me
        as I walk the streets of the city and
            mingle with its groping inhabitants.

I pray, O Lord, that You will use me,
    that through my fumbling efforts
        You will touch some soul with healing and love.

My heart is glad today, O God.
Grant that I may communicate to others
    some measure of this eternal joy.

109

O God, I have been taught to believe
    that You are God of our world.
It has been drummed into my head
    by the preachers of my youth,
    by parents, teachers, and self-appointed apostles.
"God holds the reins," they say.
"He will have the last word," they claim.

I've honestly tried to believe it.
And with tongue in cheek,
    I've sounded off to others
        about Your power and Your promises.
Maybe they sensed my disbelief.
It may be that they just habitually accepted
    or unthinkingly nodded assent
        to my platitudes and pronouncements.
How can I really believe in Your omnipotence
    unless I look the other way
        when tragedy befalls
        or close my eyes to the agony and ugliness
            on all sides of me?

I cannot believe You inflict pain on Your creatures.
I realize that our suffering is
    the consequence of our own sinful selfishness.
But what about the babies born
        with two strikes against them?
        the children killed because they're inconvenient?
    the grisly slaughter on gang turf,
        battlefield, highways?
    the diseases that kill without cause?

the destruction of thousands when the earth
    shifts and breaks under them?
the pressures and indignities
    forced on ethnic minorities?
What about this, O God?
How can I explain this to my skeptical friends
    or even to myself?

Is it possibly true, O God,
    that You really aren't omnipotent?
    that this fractured world isn't
        in the palm of Your hand?
    that Your great power is limited
        when it comes to this distorted planet
            and its sin-ridden inhabitants?

O God, the basis of all being,
    my ultimate and eternal concern,
    I know that You are not floating out there
        over and above our ball of clay.
You are in our world.
You are among Your creatures,
    inscrutable, indefinable,
        great in majesty and splendor.
You bring beauty out of ugliness.
Out of the ashes of our sickness and suffering,
    You bring forth new creations.
I never want to define You, O God,
    for I cannot worship what I comprehend.
But I pray for Your grace to stand firm
    despite my nagging doubts
    and to praise You in time of adversity.

110

God spoke to me today.
He broke through my childish doubts
    with words of comfort and assurance.
"Hang in there; sit tight;
        stick to My course for your life," He said,
    "I will not let you down."

He reminded me of how He cared for past saints,
    how He watched over them and kept them
        through their hours of suffering
            and uncertainty.
He reviewed for me my own life,
    His loving concern through the days of my youth.
He restated for me my commission and
        appointment,
    His trust in me as His servant
        in this sin-filled world.
He reiterated His gracious promises to stand by me,
    to empower and support me
        in the conflicts that await.

I know that God is with me today—
    just as surely as He was with His saints of old.
I have no reason to fear or doubt
    the eternal love and presence of my Lord.

111

My heart is full today.
I am so grateful
  for all that God has done for me.
As I crawl out of my corner
    of depression and self-pity
    and look around me, I see
      how great my God is.
I cannot see Him,
    but I can see the works of His hands.
He is a merciful and loving God.
How tenderly He deals with those
    whose hearts are open to Him!
He is a righteous and faithful God.
His promises and precepts are forever.
He is a majestic and powerful God.
He created me and sustains me day to day.
He is a forgiving God.
He takes me back to His loving heart
    when I go astray.
He is in this world today.
And those who recognize and belong to Him
    are building on foundations
      that are eternally secure.
How grateful I am to my God today!

112

What about those people who trust in God
    and are committed to His will and purposes?

They are people who are rich indeed.
Even amid the circumstances of poverty,
        the wealth and blessings of God
            are within their reach.
They are people with purpose and meaning in their lives.
Even amid the disorder and void
        of this temporal existence,
        they are aware of God's concern and love for them.
They are people who walk unafraid.
The threats of violence or prophecies of doom
        do not detract from their validity
            nor alter their course.
They are people who relate to those around them.
They identify with others
        in their sorrows and complaints
        and share with them their lives and gifts.

They are people who are truly happy
        and through whom our God works
            His purposes in this world today.

113

How great and glorious is our God!
From hour to hour, from day to day,
   our lives ought to overflow
      with praise and gratitude.
It is amazing, even fantastic,
   how our God permeates every facet of our lives
      and works His purposes
         despite our human faults and failures.

He creates beauty out of the dust
   of our fallen natures.
Out of the ashes of our failures
   He brings forth meaning and purpose.
He exalts the humble and enriches the poor.
He transforms our weaknesses
   into channels of strength.
Our emptiness becomes
   a vessel of His fullness,
   our spiritual poverty
      the basis for His eternal grace.
Our errors and mistakes
   are stepping-stones to success.
Our defeats are only incidents
   on the road to victory.

But this is God's doing, not ours.
How great and glorious is our God!

114 AND 115

We fear, O God, for our country
and the tragic indifference that is demonstrated
toward You and Your purposes.
We have built great sanctuaries and memorials
in Your honor.
We have established innumerable church bodies
that presume to glorify and serve You.
We have respectfully imprinted Your name
on our coins
and properly credited You
in our founding principles.
Our leaders generally call on You to guide them
in the most critical decisions
they must make.
A remnant of our populace gathers occasionally
to sing Your praises and profess its faith.
There are even special days
when we count our blessings
and conduct services of thanksgiving.

But the sanctuaries we build do not always glorify You.
They often become soundproof fortresses
that block out the sounds of suffering
that echo throughout the world around them.
Our numerous church bodies turn into vain attempts
to box You into human ideas
and concepts of divinity.

The coins that bear Your name are dedicated
    to the pursuit of our selfish ambitions
        and the acquisition of material wealth.
Our founding principles are interpreted to
    benefit the powerful and oppress the weak.
Our laws sometimes contradict and oppose Your law
    in the consciences and convictions
        of Your children.
Our leaders call on You to bless their intentions
    rather than to reveal Your plans
        in the way they govern.
And those who do gather to sing Your praises
    are seldom committed to anyone or anything
        unless it is comfortable and convenient
            for their purposes.

And yet, O Lord, we pray
    that You will not give up on us.
We have selfishly clutched at Your great blessings
    and abused the wealth You have put
        into our hands.
We have gathered for ourselves
    while countless millions
        of this world's creatures have died
            with their needs unfulfilled.
We have foolishly ignored You to worship the things
    that have come from Your hands.

We confess our rebelliousness and selfishness,
O Lord,
and pray that You will spare us.
Spare us that you might renew us
and save us
and use us to share Your blessings
with Your human creatures in every land.
You dealt mercifully with Your ungrateful children
throughout history.
We pray that You will deal patiently and lovingly
with us,
that You will transform our words into actions
and our shallow platitudes into genuine praises
that will glorify and serve You
in all the world.

116

I know that God is here.
I know this because,
    with my soul bare and my body naked before Him,
    He looked on me with love
        and responded to my cry for help.

There was a time when I didn't care!
I was not aware of any particular need for Him.
But then I hit bottom.
Death itself reached out to embrace me.
There was no one else to turn to.
I cried out to God in my desperation.
I could almost feel His invisible hand
    encircle me and draw me to Himself.

Now I am convinced.
God is here, and I shall trust Him forever.
I will no longer wait for pain or suffering
    to drive me to Him.
I will walk in His course for my life.
I am committed to His purposes,
    and I intend to carry out that commitment.

I can never repay God for His ever-present love.
I can only dedicate my life to praising Him
    and to serving Him wherever I may be.
I am His servant and His child; I shall love Him forever.
I shall proclaim to all the world: "God is in our midst."

117 AND 118

O God, I am thoroughly frightened when I see
　　the things that are happening around me.
And when I dare to peer into the future,
　　I become very nervous as I consider
　　　　what may happen to me and my world.

I do remember Your many promises.
I keep telling myself:
　　　"With the Lord on my side,
　　　I do not have to be afraid;
　　what can anyone do to me?"
But when I see the old foundations crumbling
　　　and the old certainties
　　　and securities giving way,
　　I feel as if I am falling with no one
　　　　to catch me
　　or that my ship has broken loose
　　　from its anchor, leaving me
　　　　at the mercy of a tempestuous sea.

Our world has slipped its moorings:
　　　our population threatens to overwhelm us;
　　　our waste products are about to smother us;
　　　our modern weapons are capable
　　　　of obliterating us;
　　　diseases run rampant, claiming
　　　　innocent lives.
Because we are incapable of loving and living
　　　　for one another,

we are about to be destroyed
by our own self-centeredness
and to turn the beautiful world You have given us
into a wasted and desolate planet.
It all seems so unreal,
and I feel so small and insignificant
in such a world.
And sometimes it seems, O God,
that even You have left us to our own devices
and have given us up for lost.
Or, I wonder, are You about to wind up history?
Is Your purpose for our world
about to be consummated?

You do speak to my fears, O Lord.
You offer no guarantees
about the future of the world,
but You have assured me that my status
as Your beloved child is eternal.
Whatever happens to my world,
You will never let me go.
You have set me free from fear
and will keep me safe and secure
through all the storms
that rage around me.
You are my God;
whatever happens to the world,
I will celebrate Your love forever.

119

O God, I want so much to please You,
  to walk in Your ways
  and to carry out Your purposes.
Nothing is as important to me
    as being in the center of Your will
      and living within Your design for my life.

While others may find their fulfillment
    in the acquisition of wealth
      or the accumulation of things,
    in doing something better than everyone else,
      or in the plaudits of their peers,
    my foremost desire is
      to be the object of Your love
      and to be Your child and servant forever.

Not only have You fashioned me with Your hands,
    O Lord,
    and created me for Your purposes,
    You have stamped Your image on my heart.
Therefore my deepest longings are met only in You
    and in the dedication of my life
      to the accomplishment of Your objectives.

How can I live a life that is pleasing to You,
    O Lord?
My instincts are earthbound.
The transitory delights of this life
    tantalize and tempt me.
My insatiable longings
    and desperate attempts to please You
      are thwarted by the innumerable
      enemies of my soul.

I fail so often to do what I really want to do,
  to attain what I strive for,
  to grasp what I reach for,
and I fall back in shame
  and am flattened in despair.

You do forgive me when I fail, O Lord,
  and You set me on my feet again.
You have promised to strengthen me
  and to sustain me in my daily conflicts.
Now I pray for the wisdom to discern Your will
  and the grace to carry it out
    in the difficult days before me.
You have shown me how much You love me, Lord;
  now show me how to love You.
Your standards for me are clear.
I am to translate Your love into terms
    that others can comprehend,
  to demonstrate it before my fellow beings.
I can truly love You only as I proceed
  to love Your children in this world.
I can serve You only as I commit my life to service
  on behalf of my brothers and sisters.
I can offer sacrifices to You only as
  I sacrifice to meet my neighbor's need.
This is Your law and standard,
  Your design and will for my life.
This is the way in which I will be pleasing to You.

I do love You, O God,
  and Your will for me is the delight of my heart.
I have a sincere love for many people
    who cross my path,
  and I rejoice in the privilege of serving them.

And yet, O Lord, there are so many people
    whom I do not love.
The demons of bigotry and apathy,
    jealousy and selfishness,
        plague my soul and numb my sensitivities.
They stay my hand from reaching out
    to help others.
I sin against You when I sin against them,
    and I need to be restored and renewed
        by Your loving touch.

How I praise You, O Lord,
    because You love me even when I fail
        to respond in loving obedience!
Whereas I cannot comprehend You,
    You do understand me,
    and You continue to hold me
        within Your loving embrace.
While I fall short of my sincere intentions
        to abide within Your will for me,
    Your promises are eternally secure,
    and You tenderly and patiently
        rekindle the fires within me and empower me
        to do that which I cannot do by myself.

I love You, O God,
    and I gladly accept Your will and purpose
        for my life.
Now bless me and guide me
    and grant me the grace
    to walk within Your will and purpose
    and have the joy of knowing
        that I am pleasing to You.

120

I am distressed, O Lord,
    by the attitudes and actions of those
        who claim to honor Your name
            and to live within Your purposes.

They don't really listen to Your Word.
They appear to be following some other god,
    or they are simply taking the path
        of least resistance.
They assume that their wishes are Your will,
    that the crowd they travel with
    or the nations that govern them
        are righteously carrying out Your objectives
            despite their ungodly
                means and methods.

How long, O Lord, must I dwell
    in a world that breeds violence
    and amongst people that engage in war?

Teach me, O God, how to be a peacemaker,
    how to confront violence with love,
    how to courageously and patiently promote
        Your will and Your Word
            among the hostile and angry masses.

121

Where should I look for help in my need?
To majestic mountain peaks that probe our skies
    or to giants of industry that clog our land?
To satellites that circle our world
    or to computers that store our knowledge?

The answer to my problems
    and the fulfillment of my needs
must come from God Himself,
    from Him who created skies and mountains
    and men and women to dwell in their midst.
He is a great God who knows our every desire,
    whose watchful eye is upon us night and day.
We can make no move without His knowledge.
His concern for His children is constant,
    His love for them eternal.

And thus the Lord will keep you,
    shielding you from the forces of evil
    as a shade tree shields you
        from the rays of the blazing sun.

He does care for you,
    and He will fight with you
        against the enemies of your soul.
Whether you are coming or going,
    He knows the course you take,
        and He will go before you.

122 AND 123

How good it is to enter the sanctuary of the Lord!
I know that God is not confined
within our four-walled creations,
nor is He attached to altars and brass symbols.
And yet, in the beauty and quietness of God's house,
I find His presence very real and fulfilling.

God is with me and around me
even as I make my way
through the concrete and steel jungles
of the cold and unfriendly city.

He is present even behind the anonymous faces
of the rushing crowds elbowing their way
to their respective destinations.
I find Him in the hearts and lives of His children
who infiltrate the masses
and run His errands
and fulfill His purposes
in the course of their daily duties.
I cannot outrun or evade my God.
He goes before me and follows closely behind me.
He will keep me and sustain me wherever I am.

And yet I rejoice as I enter His sanctuary
and mingle with those who honor His name
and seek His grace.

There, shielded from the screaming tensions
and ear-splitting sounds of the city,
in the company of those who love one another,
I happily open my heart
to the loving mercy of God.

124 AND 125

What cowards we are,
  we who claim to be the sons and daughters of God!
How insipid is our faith
  in an insecure and faithless world!
The pressures increase.
The old props fall away.
Many of the old traditions and standards
  we held so dear are no longer relevant
    in our rapidly changing society.
Even the proclamations and exhortations,
  the prophecies and promises,
    that excited and supported us in our youth
    sound hollow and empty and frightfully
    inadequate in these times in which we live.
The little boxes we wrapped around our God
  are breaking up;
    we can no longer hold on to Him in our
    expanding, exploding universe.

Though we cannot hold on to God,
  He does hold on to us.
Those who trust in the true God are more secure
  than the great mountains that rise above the
    clouds that cover us.
Though everything changes around us,
  our great God cannot be changed.

194

Though the sands may shift and
   even our institutions and governments
   and the ideals and aspirations of
      men and women give way,
   our great God is not subject to the impermanence
   of our temporal world.
Though the storm sweeps over us,
   our relationship with our loving God is forever.

What cowards we are, we who claim to be the
   sons and daughters of God!
We don't have to be afraid.
Let us have faith in God!

126

Let us begin this day with rejoicing!
Let us acknowledge our Lord's love and concern
　　and allow our bodies to break forth
　　　　into happy hilarity!
Let us give our nerves and muscles
　　the healthy exercise of laughter!
The Lord has done such wonderful things for us;
　　let us be glad!

The day before us is uncertain.
We don't know what we will encounter on our way.
While we rejoice with those who rejoice,
　　we shall also weep with those who suffer.
While we may be surprised by heavenly bliss,
　　we may also pass through corridors of darkness.
Wherever we go, we go forth as children and servants
　　of the living God,
　　　　and we go forth to touch the lives of men and women
　　　　　　with His healing love.
Let us begin this day with rejoicing
　　and return to our homes with gladness!

127 AND 128

Those human creatures who struggle for
 significance
 apart from God's will and purposes
 struggle in vain.
They build homes and institutions;
 they acquire property and possessions;
 they crowd the land with their clutter
 of questionable achievements;
 they fill the better part of every day
 with self-centered activities;
 they strive constantly to get to the top.
And all the while, worth and value
 are within their reach or very close to them.
They possess a precious gift from God
 that comes in some measure to all people.

There are visible evidences of a man and woman's worth:
 the children they beget,
 their ability to supply their family's needs
 through daily labor.
But even beyond this and long before this,
 a person's true worth was established
 by God Himself.

129

O God, I get awfully tired of static.
I am fed up with the flack that comes my way
    from those I am trying to serve.
It seems that they suspect or misinterpret
        or question my motives or authority
            in everything I do or say.
I think people enjoy putting me down.
I just can't get them off my back.

Do I have to constantly live
    with this sort of thing, O Lord?
What about this joy that is promised to those
    who are Your servants and ministers?

Forgive me for my unworthy thoughts, O Lord.
Overlook my vicious complaints.
    Fill my heart with Your love
        so I will respond in love
            even toward those who do not love me.
Enable me, O Lord, to find my joy in You
    and to reflect that joy to the unresponsive,
        reactionary, disagreeable people
            who do not like me very much.

O God, tonight I seek You
 with a heart full of guilt
 and a mind full of bewilderment
  and frustration.
You have heard me before
 and responded with grace and mercy.
Now I seek You again.

I know I am guilty, O God.
But if You kept account of people's
  failings and fallings,
  no one could ever face You.
I reach for You
  because You look with loving mercy
  on my wretched soul.
You will accept me and forgive me
  and reinstate me in Your purposes.

It is no wonder that I return again and again to God.
I long for His forgiveness and acceptance
  more than the night watchman longs
  for the dawn of day.

Thus I plead with you to focus your faith on God.
You will find love there—and salvation.
And He will cleanse you of your sin
  and restore you to His loving heart.

131

O God, I have failed
  because I expected too much of myself.
I have fallen
    because I focused too much on success
      and reckoned too little with my own humanity.

It is time that I still my restless heart
    and quiet my overambitious spirit.

It is far better that I center my aspirations
    on God and His will for my life.

132

We remember, O Lord,
    those past saints who suffered sorely
      on Your behalf.
In obedience to You, they endured persecution—
    even torture and death.
In their heroic determination to live by Your will
      and to remain in Your course for their lives,
    they proclaimed and demonstrated Your Word
      to this world's masses.

We remember, O Lord,
    and we are ashamed of our insipid faith,
      our cowardice,
        our fear of offending those with power over us
        and of being despised by those around us.

Make us aware, O Lord,
    of Your children who even today
    are suffering for their faith,
    who even in our great country
      have the courage to place Your will
        above the laws of the state
      and are subjected to
        the indignities of imprisonment,
        the scorn of their peers,
        and even the compassionless criticisms
    of many of us who honor Your name.

We confess, O Lord,
      our lack of courage and understanding.
We pray for Your blessing on those who suffer,
      that You will not forget them
         in their hour of trial
      and that You will not turn Your face from them
         in their lonely hours of doubt and pain.

Visit them with joy; empower them with Your Spirit;
      watch over and care for them.
May the influence of their courageous convictions
      shake us out of our lethargy,
         move us from the fringes of fear and indecision
         into the center of Your will.
      Empower us with Your grace
         to carry on Your purposes
            despite the consequences
            that may come our way.

133 AND 134

O God, how precious it is for us
and how pleasing it must be to You
when Your children and servants learn
how to live and work together in unity!

It is in the measure that we do this
that we begin to resemble You
and to carry out more effectively Your purposes
in our disjointed and discordant world.
Come, let us bless His name together,
rejoice in His loving concern for us,
declare His worth to all creatures,
and walk in obedience to His will.

The same God made heaven and earth
and all of us who dwell here.
Let us worship and serve Him together.

135

Despite the depressing conditions of our world
    and the distortions of our society,
        or even the problems and conflicts of our lives,
    let us take time to praise the Lord.

We who gather for services of worship,
    let us come together to celebrate God's presence
        and to praise Him for His great gifts.
As we take our place in our workday world,
    let us begin by praising the Lord.
When we meet with our family and friends,
    let us unite our voices in praises to the Lord.
Farmers who labor alone with the soil and seed
        can praise God
            who brings forth the fruit.
Office workers who mingle with the masses
        that impersonally jostle them
    and work amid the tall structures
        that belittle them
    can praise God who knows
        and loves them forever.
Without our God to praise and worship and serve,
    there is no real purpose in life,
        no meaning, no identity, and no reason
            for existing in this cold, calculating world.
You who are on beds of pain,
    even you have reason to praise the Lord.
You who are left to die in homes for the aged,
    you, too, can find purpose
        in praising the Lord.

When you feel you are forgotten,
   your loving God never forgets.
When you are tired and lonely,
   your great God will never leave your side.

Those people who have no God to praise,
      who neglect to come before
         their Creator and Redeemer,
      are like creatures wandering in darkness.
They focus on the fitful, fleeing things
      of this life.
Like butterflies over a flower bed,
      they flutter from blossom to blossom,
         getting their pollen wherever they can.
Then they return to their beds
      only to await the meaningless existence
      of another day.

God is available—to be recognized and praised.
He has reached out to His lost children
      to lovingly draw them to Himself.
He gives them identity and purpose,
      a name and a goal,
      and makes them
         eternally secure and significant.

Let us praise the Lord!
He makes our lives and our living,
         every hour and every day, truly worthwhile;
      and we belong to Him forever.

136

Thank You, God,
    for all these things that reveal Your love.
Thank You for the heavens that cover us,
       for the earth beneath our feet,
       for the sun in the day and the stars in the night,
       for the snow and the rains,
       for mountains and valleys and trees and flowers.

Thank You, God,
    for those people who demonstrate Your love.
Thank You for those great men and women who
       followed You throughout history,
       for the priests and prophets
         and apostles and ministers,
       for doctors and teachers and mothers and fathers
         and painters and musicians and writers
         and farmers and laborers and clerks,
       for those men and women who gloried in Your love
         and dedicated their lives
         to loving others.

Thank You, God,
    for choosing me to be one of Your people,
    for calling me and equipping me to communicate
       Your love to the world around me.
Thank You, God.

137

How grateful we are, O God,
  for our great country
  for the blessings You lavish on our land.
How concerned we are, O Lord,
  that our nation may become our god
  and that we worship the gifts
    rather than the Giver!

Is it possible, O God,
  that our laws may circumvent Your will?
  that our freedom may place chains on others?
  that our wealth may impoverish someone?
  that our power may come
    at the expense of another's weakness?
  that our enemies may be those
    who are obedient to You?

Dare we pray, O God,
  that You take away those things that come
    between us and You?
  that You raise up men and women who will oppose
    those institutions and those citizens
    who carelessly, even unconsciously,
    equate patriotism with allegiance to You?

We pray, O God,
  that our nation may be restored to Your objectives
  and that Your children who live in this land
    may dedicate their lives to You and Your purposes.

138

I am exceedingly grateful, O Lord,
   for You have heard my cries and complaints,
   and You responded with mercy and strength.
Now my life is overflowing with thanksgiving,
   and my mouth is filled with Your praises.

If only the leaders of our disjointed world
      would listen to Your words
      and direct their people in accord with Your will.
Then they would know the meaning of peace,
   and they would rejoice in the ways of God.

You have not shielded me
      from the pains of trouble
         or the ravages of conflict,
   but You have kept me
      even amid sorrow and suffering.
You take my side against the enemies of my soul,
   and You will not allow them to destroy me.

Thus I know You will fulfill Your purpose for my life.
Your love and mercy are everlasting;
   You will not let me go.

139 🌿

O God, You know me inside and out,
   through and through.
Everything I do,
         every thought that flits through my mind,
         every step I take,
         every plan I make,
         every word I speak,
      You know, even before these things happen.
You know my past;
      You know my future.
Your enveloping presence covers my every move.
Your knowledge of me sometimes comforts me,
      sometimes frightens me,
         but it is always far beyond my comprehension.

There is no way to escape You, no place to hide.
If I ascend to the heights of joy,
      You are there before me.
If I plunge into the depths of despair,
      You are there to meet me.
I could fly to the other side of the world
      and find You there to lead the way.
I could walk into the darkest night,
      only to find You there
         to lighten its dismal hours.

You were present at my conception.
You guided the molding of my unformed members
      within the body of my mother.

Nothing about me, from beginning to end,
     has been hidden from Your eyes.
How frightfully, fantastically wonderful it all is!

May Your all-knowing, everywhere-present Spirit
     continue to search out my feelings and thoughts.
Deliver me
     from that which may hurt or destroy me,
     and guide me along the paths of love and truth.

140

O God, deliver our nation and our world
    from those people in positions of authority
        who resort to violence
        to carry out their objectives.
They sweet-talk us into believing
        they are acting in our interests
    and brainwash us into blind,
        flag-waving allegiance
until we march by their side
        into battles that destroy
        our unity and joy as members of
        the human family.

Deliver all of us, O Lord,
        from the notion that anything of value or worth
        can be obtained by hostile or violent actions.

Our God is on the side of those who are afflicted.
He will deal justly with people who are violent,
        and show His mercy to the victims
        of their obscene actions.

Help us, O Lord,
        even at the risk of our lives and well-being,
    to overcome hate with love
    and to be peacemakers in a world
        that is so racked and distorted
        by the atrocities of violence.

141

O God, I come to You in sorrow and shame.
I spoke up in my own defense today
    and uttered words that knifed their way
        into the heart of my friend,
    and this created a great rift between us.
I would never raise my hand to strike anybody,
    but the tongue is more destructive than the fist,
    and I hurt the one I love.

Heal the hurt of my friend, O Lord,
    and heal the sickness within my heart
        that forced my foolish tongue
        into such irresponsible actions.

I come to claim Your loving mercy.
I pray, as well, that you grant my friend
    the grace to forgive me.
May Your Spirit who abides in my heart
    curb and control my rebellious tongue
    and teach me to speak words
        that give life and promote love
        in this hate-ridden world.

142

I direct my cries to the Lord.
Out of the ear-piercing sounds and
     ceaseless turmoil of this concrete jungle,
   I speak God's name.
For my heart is deeply troubled and depressed,
     and I feel weary and faint.

I am confused and lost.
I cannot find my way.
The nameless faces that flit by
     take no notice of me.
No one knows my name,
     and no one cares.

I turn to You, O God.
You have heard me before,
     and You responded to my cries.
Perhaps even amid the frustrating activity
       and crowded streets of this great land,
     You can hear the cries of a lonely child.

O God, deliver me from my prison of loneliness.
Turn my cries of distress
     into proclamations of joy.
Direct my steps into the fellowship
     of others who love and serve You.

143

It was another one of those days, Lord,
    when I should have stayed in bed.
Everything I attempted to do was headed for failure.
I honestly tried to show concern for others,
    but I got cold shoulders in return.
I tried to speak words of comfort,
    and they were thrown back into my teeth.
I wanted to do well at my job,
    but it seemed I just got in everybody's way.

Sometimes it just isn't worth it, Lord,
    and I wonder if it isn't time to fold up
        and shove off in search of greener pastures.
I want desperately to be a success,
    to add points to my score,
    or to get commended now and then.
But this didn't happen today, Lord,
    and it happens so seldom, I wonder what's wrong.
Am I following Your course for my life,
    or am I just muddling through
        without purpose or design?

I need You, God, now more than ever before.
And if I don't get some special lift,
    some sense of Your support and encouragement,
    I will go right down the tube.

Come closer, O Lord, that I may hear again
    Your voice of comfort and concern.

144

O God, it is difficult to understand
    how You can hold Your creatures in such high regard
    and show them such concern.
Their years on this earth are so few.
They are little more than a wisp of wind
    in the time and space of Your great universe.

You created them as the objects of Your love—
    only to see them turn from You
    to play with their foolish toys.
You tried to teach them to love their fellow beings—
    only to see them express
      their fears and suspicion and hate
    through cruel acts of violence and war.
You showered on them Your abundant gifts—
    only to see them make these gifts their
      ultimate concern.

Still You continue to love them
    and seek continuously to save them
      from destroying themselves and the world
      You have placed in their hands.
Even while they reject You,
    You reach out to draw them back to Yourself.
Even while they suffer the painful consequences
    of rank rebelliousness,
    You offer to them Your healing
      and demonstrate Your desire
      to restore them to love and joy.

And when they finally turn to You,
　　they find You waiting for them,
　　　　ready to forgive their sins and to welcome them
　　　　to Your life and purposes once more.

Those who return to their Lord are happy indeed!
They will forever be the objects
　　of God's love and blessings.

145

God is here—let's celebrate!
Let us enlist our lives in continuous celebration
of God's goodness and greatness.
Let us announce to the world God's presence
and proclaim His loving concern for all His creatures.
How compassionate He is toward all He has created,
how tender toward His failure-fraught creatures!
He will not back out on His promises to us.
His blessings are not reserved only for those
who fit obediently into His design for them.
He is just—and He is forgiving.
He gently picks up those who have fallen
and restores them to Himself.
He sustains those who are wavering in weakness
and grants them His grace and strength.
He reaches into the void of empty lives
and enriches and fulfills their hungry hearts.
He is near enough to hear our every cry,
to sense our every need,
to grant us whatever is necessary
to make us happy and productive
as we seek to follow and to serve Him.

How incomparably glorious is our great God!
May our mouths articulate and our lives demonstrate
His ever-present love for all His creatures!
Let us celebrate
the eternal mercy and goodness of our God!

146

Praise God!
As long as I have breath in my body,
　　I will praise God!

Don't pin your hopes on the genius of men or women.
Their ultimate end is the same as yours,
　　and they become once more
　　　　like the dust from which they came.

Those who draw their strength from God are secure.
He who created the earth and all upon it
　　is the only One who can heal the wounds
　　and mend the fractures of our disjointed world.
He can break the bonds of obsession
　　and pierce humanity's stupor with visions of truth.
He tenderly reaches out
　　to those who are oppressed
　　and reveals His concern
　　　　for those who are lost and lonely.
He watches over His own
　　while the paths of the godless
　　　　lead to their own destruction.

This is the God who cannot die!
Praise God!
Amen!

147 THROUGH 150

How good it is to celebrate God's presence
   and to sing His praises throughout each day!
We celebrate what He has done for His children
      through history:
      His creation of our world
         and the sun and the moon and
         the unnumbered stars
      that light up our universe;
      His creatures that swim and crawl
         and walk and fly on our planet;
      His children chosen to enjoy
         these great gifts around them.
We praise Him for dealing with His human creatures
      through His blessings heaped upon them;
      His revelations through signs and wonders;
      His tender love and gentle concern
         in His care shown toward them.
We praise Him for His devoted servants:
      who communicated His Word;
      who performed His miracles;
      who brought His healing to people's hurts.
We celebrate His continued blessings to our world:
      the flowers that bloom in glorious color;
      the rains that freshen the earth;
      the birds that fill the air with song.

We give thanks for His perpetual love:
    His forgiveness of our sins;
    His pursuit of those who run from Him;
    His reaching out to heal them
    and to draw them to Himself.

We call all men and women to praise the Lord:
    those who preach to proclaim His love;
    those who sing to glorify His name;
    those who can shout or whistle
      or write or paint
      or dance or play musical instruments
    or pound on drums or ring bells
      to join in celebrating
    the majesty of our great and loving God.

3 9371 00021 6473

BS 1440 .B73 1996
Brandt, Leslie F.
Psalms/now

DATE DUE			

CONCORDIA UNIVERSITY LIBRARY
2811 NE Holman St.
Portland, OR 97211